Warrior 101

A Spiritual Warfare Training Manual for Active Duty

Written and Developed

By

Bishop Dr. Jackie L. Green, D. Min.

Equipping the Saints for Everyday Battles with Biblical Battle Strategies

Published by

JGM-Enternational Prayer Life Institute, Redlands, California

OUR VISION

The JGM-National PrayerLife Institute is a non-profit national and international Christian organization dedicated and commissioned to raising up healthy houses of prayer around the world, equipping saints for the work of the ministry, and fulfilling the Great Commission in cooperation with the larger Body of Jesus Christ.

OUR PURPOSE

TRANSFORMING AND BUILDING LIVES, CHURCHES, CITIES, AND NATIONS

THROUGH PRAYER

Matthew 21:12-14, Ephesians 4:11-16, Matthew 28:18-20, Psalms 2:8

Warrior 101

A Spiritual Warfare Training Manual for Active Duty

Equipping the Saints for Everyday Battles with Biblical Battle Strategies
© Copyright 2011, by Bishop Dr. Jackie L. Green

Published by JGM-Enternational Prayer Life Institute, Redlands, CA

ALL RIGHTS RESERVED. This book is protected under the copyright laws of the United States of America. This book may not be copied or reprinted for commercial gain or profit. Contents may not be reproduced in whole or in part, in any form or by any means without written permission from the publisher.

ADDITIONAL COPIES MAY BE ORDERED THROUGH

JGM-NATIONAL PRAYERLIFE INSTITUTE

420 East Stuart Avenue, Redlands, CA 92374

Visit our Website at www.jgmenternational.org **and** raphadeliveranceuniv.org

This Teaching Manual is

Dedicated to

OUR GOD WHO IS CALLED

"A MAN OF WAR"

Exodus 15:3

And to a New Generation of

Spiritual Warriors and Prayer Warriors

Arising in the 21st Century

Course Objectives

WARRIOR 101

1. To build and equip believers in the knowledge and strategies of spiritual warfare in everyday life.

2. To study the battles of the Bible and apply those strategies to everyday life.

3. To identify and equip leaders and believers to deal with our personal and corporate enemies.

4. To study and learn about the devices and strategies of (Satan), the enemy of God and the Church.

5. To raise up spiritual warriors through spiritual disciplines, strategies and a greater level of discernment in the Body of Christ.

6. To train spiritual warriors, leaders and ministries/churches how to become a Warrior Church and choose their battles wisely

7. To increase their spiritual weapons and arsenal of spiritual strategies for the battles

8. To build up the Kingdom of God and tear down the Kingdoms of darkness.

9. To activate the "warrior spirit" on the inside of every believer to become more than conquerors and win daily battles as well as triumph in Kingdom warfare for the souls of cities and nations and the souls of men, women, boys and girls.

10. Equip the saints in the use of key scriptures as spiritual weapons of warfare *which are not carnal* but mighty through God to pull down strongholds

TEXTBOOKS;

The Holy Bible (Choose your own Bible version)

Text Book: Battles of the Bible, A Military History of Ancient Israel by Chaim Herzog and Mordechai Gichon

Student Registration

Student Notebook/Syllabus

WEEKLY REVIEW QUIZZES AND FINAL EXAM

RAPHA DELIVERANCE UNIVERSITY --CREDITS: 3 Credit Units

Student must attend 10 Classes out of 12 to receive full credit and must take final exam.

GRADING SYSTEM: Attendance 30%,

Class Participation 30% , Final Exam -40% of Grade

Warrior 101- Course Outline

Week 1- Introduction- No Cowards in the Kingdom..7

Week 2- Know Your Enemy...18

Week 3- Satan's Harassment Plan and How to Torment the Enemy...............................29

Week 4- How to Fight an Invisible Enemy..40

Week 5- Joshua, The Conquering Warrior- Battles of Joshua...46

Week 6- Night Warrior and Night Warfare...54

Week 7- Nehemiah- A Night Warrior..59

Week 8- Wounded Warriors by *Apostle Ivory Hopkins*...64

Week 9- Samson-Weekend Warrior (*Losing the Battle Behind Closed Doors*)...............75

Week 10- How Warriors Are Chosen(Gideon)...85

Week 11- Wise Warriors: Taking Territory Little by Little..90

Take Home Final Exam due next week...94

Week 12- Becoming A Warrior Church..97

Prophetic Word to the Warrior Church 103

APPENDIX

Warrior Scriptures..105

Suggested Reading List..110

About the Author..115

Warrior Lesson 1--Introduction

NO COWARDS IN THE KINGDOM

Welcome to Warrior 101. The calling of God to the warriors today is expressed very well in the song lyrics below. Play the song if you have it or choose readers to declare the lyrics with a drum beat in the background. Enjoy your journey to "Warriorhood in Christ."

Rita Springer - Holy Visitation Lyrics

Sound the alarm, gather the people
Gather the elders, let the ministers wail
God, take back the years that the enemy's stolen
Lord, You are coming with the Holy Visitation

Sound the alarm and awaken the watchmen
Open their ears, let their voices be loud
We prophecy, You'll come to this nation
Touch this generation with a Holy Visitation

We return to You
With fasting and weeping and mourning
Oh, my Lord, You're returning
We lie here weeping between porch and altar
Pour out Your spirit on Your sons and Your daughters

Sound the alarm and awaken the watchmen
Open their ears, let their voices be loud
We prophecy, You'll come to this nation
Touch this generation with a Holy Visitation

We return to You
With fasting and weeping and mourning
Oh, my Lord, You're returning
We lie here weeping between porch and altar
Pour out Your spirit on Your sons and Your daughters

We dance and we shout and we lift up our voice
Let your kingdom come down
We dance and we shout and we lift up our voice
Let your kingdom come down

We return to You
With fasting and weeping and mourning
Oh, my Lord, You're returning
We lie here weeping between porch and altar
Pour out Your spirit on Your sons and Your daughters
We lie here weeping between porch and altar
Pour out Your spirit on Your sons and Your daughters

[Rita Springer Lyrics are found on www.songlyrics.com]
We dance and we shout and we lift up our voice
Let your kingdom come down
We dance and we shout and we lift up our voice
Let your kingdom come down

And we dance 'cause I was made for war
And I was made for battle, Lord
And I was made for war
I was made for battle, Lord

I was made for war
I was made for battle, Lord
I was made for war
I was made for battle, Lord

Release the cries
Release the broken
Release the captive love
We return to you, we return to you, we return to you

We lie here weeping between porch and altar
Pour it out, pour it out, pour it out over Your sons and Your daughters
Pour it out, pour it out, pour it out over Your sons and Your daughters

We prophecy, You'll come to this nation
We prophecy, You'll touch this generation
Awaken the watchmen Lord
Awaken the watchmen God

Getting to Know the Warriors

Name Your Battles Survey

(Check off all that apply to your present battles in life. Share with the class.)

____abuse and violence	____education	____poverty
____addictions	____emotions	____unforgiveness
____aging	____ex-spouse/friend	____wounded spirit
____anger management	____family issues	____witchcraft
____bills	____friendships	____widowhood
____business (marketplace)	____finances	____relationships
____Cancer	____future	____oppression
____Career	____God	____self (flesh)
____church issues	____health	____fear (s)
____children	____mental health	____peace of mind
____chronic illness	____money	____Other
____death	____litigation/law suits	_____
____debts	____incarceration	_____
____demonic issues	____loneliness	_____
____depression	____singleness	_____
____disabilities	____Widowhood	_____
____diet/overweight	____My past	
____divorce/separation	____unemployment	
____dreams and visions	____territorial warfare	
____eating habits	____pain	

Introductory Lesson

No Cowards in the Kingdom

"But cowards, unbelievers, the corrupt, murderers, the immoral, those who practice witchcraft, idol worshipers and all liars-their fate is in the fiery lake of burning sulfur. This is the second death." Revelation 21:8

"We are not born as "warriors" but we come into the earth realm as somewhat of a "coward." It is not until we surrender our lives to Christ and are filled with His Holy Spirit that we become fit for the Master's use. Before you become a true warrior for Christ, you will have to give up your old nature and the tendency to be a coward when faced the Devil and all the trials and tribulations that life can bring." *(Bishop Jackie Green)*

Definition: *What is a* **Coward?**

_____

_____

_____

Key Text: II Timothy 1:7

"For God has not given us a spirit of fear and timidity, but of power, love, and self discipline." (NLT)

Key Text: Luke 22:56-62

"A servant girl noticed him in the firelight and began staring at him. Finally she said, "This man was one of Jesus' followers!" 57 But Peter denied it. "Woman," he said, "I don't even know him!" 58 After a while someone else looked at him and said, "You must be one of them!"

"No, man, I'm not! Peter retorted. 59 About an hour later someone else insisted, "This must be one of them, because he is a Galilean, too." 60 But Peter said, "man, I don't know what you are talking about." And immediately, while he was still speaking, the rooster crowed. 61 At that moment the Lord turned and look at Peter. Suddenly, the Lord's words flashed through Peter's mind. "Before the rooster crows tomorrow morning, you will deny three times that you even know me." 62 And Peter left the courtyard, weeping bitterly.

Share with the group reasons why Peter turned coward:

1. _____
2. _____
3. _____
4. _____

Share why you feel Peter wept after being a coward.

1. _____
2. _____
3. _____
4. _____
5. _____
6. _____
7. _____

Satan is a Bully So You had Better Learn to Fight!

Getting to Know You

Group Work

1. Share with the class your first fight as a kid. Did you win? Who taught you how to fight?

2. Were you ever a bully? Share with the class.

3. Now read the article on Bullies.

How to Deal With Bullying The Positive Ways

1. Tell someone: Listen to your child and understand the problem:
   Before coming up with a strategy, listen to your child to describe the bullies, the bullying acts, and extent of the problems. Ask proper questions to probe your child for proper answers.

2. Evaluate the extent of the bullying:
   After you understand the situation, evaluate what actions should be taken. If it involves serious violent acts, it becomes a criminal matter and you must report it to the police and school immediately to protect your child. If not, then work with your child to come up with a strategy.

3. Face the problem:
   The worst thing is to teach your child to take the insult or not do anything. It will hurt your child's confidence and self-esteem. Instead, teach your child tackle the problem head on. Granted that you should not teach your child to go after the bully. At the same time, don't tell your child to avoid the bully.

4. Help you child solve the problem by himself or herself:
   As parents we are tempted to solve all problems for our kids, resist the temptation is the better option, enabling your child to learn to be independent and develop survival skills early on.

Therefore, avoid rushing to beat up the bully or yell at the bully's parents immediately. Let your child handle it instead.

5. Teach your child to handle verbal abuse:
Teach your child not to get angry with verbal abuse (this is not easy). Respond with the truth. Tell the bully to stop anything untruthful. If the verbal abuses continue, ask the bully why he or she is doing that. The key here is to confront the bully. If everything fails, just walk away.

6. Confront and fight back:
Bullies like to pick on those who are quiet. Teach your child to confront the bully directly. Tell them to stop. Teach your child to say "I am not afraid of you" Or "Stop being so childish." Ironically, confronting the bullies would sometimes make them respect your child more.

7. Act cool:
Sometimes bullies would feel stupid if they try to tease you but you ignore them. In other words, if your child remains cool and ignore silly remarks and gestures, then the bullies might lose interest with your child.

8. Stick with friends:
Bullies like to pick on isolated kids. Teach your child to stick with a few friends during recess and lunch. Help your child make a few friends by actively scheduling play date and getting to know other parents. Your child will feel stronger being with a few good friends.

9. Get involved in anti-bullying activities:
Knowledge is power. Get involved in the anti-bullying campaign in school. The more you know the stronger you will be in

dealing with bullying. You will also likely to get more attention from the school authority as an active participant.

Read more: How to Deal With Bullying The Positive Ways | eHow.com http://www.ehow.com/how_5235851_deal-bullying-positive-ways.html#ixzz1Dxejdbcr

From these principles on bullies, we can see spiritual implications also as we deal with the Devil daily.

GROUP WORK

Break up in groups and turn the nine principles we just read into spiritual principles as spiritual warriors.

Example:

1. Pray and tell the Lord about it and then tell someone you trust when you are going through a spiritual battle with the Devil. Don't try to handle it alone. The Devil is out to kill, steal and destroy. (*Jeremiah 33:3 and John 10:10*)

2.

3.

4.

5.

6.

7.

8.

9.

A bully will often pick on someone they view as weaker than themselves. Remember Satan is a bully and a liar too.

Share seven ways the enemy (Satan) is bullying you or people that that you know.

1._____
2._____
3._____
4._____
5._____
6._____
7._____

(Read this prayer daily for the next week)

Warrior 101 Prayer of Dedication

Dear Heavenly Father, You are Jehovah Sabaoth, the Lord of Hosts, and there is none above you. You are Lord over the armies of heaven. Father, I surrender my life to you to serve you all the days of my life. *Teach my hands to war and my fingers to fight.* Blessed be the name of the Lord, for I will win each battle in His might. For you are my goodness, my shelter, my strong tower and my shield. You are my deliverer and you will cause me to triumph in every life situation. And even when Satan, the accuser comes to bully me and to intimidate me, I know you have not given me the spirit of fear, but a spirit of power, love and a sound mind.

Forgive me Lord and I repent when I have acted like a coward. Fill me with our precious Holy Spirit so that the spirit of boldness and authority will come upon me. For I know the Kingdom of God is in power and not just a lot of talk.

I declare that I will fight the good fight of faith for I am not called to be a coward but a conqueror. *I am more than a conqueror in Christ Jesus*, and I am ready to taste the grapes and no longer afraid of the giants that are sent my way. I will not walk in fear, but I declare from Psalms 27 that you are my light and my salvation so why should I be afraid? You are my fortress and You will protect me from danger, so why should I tremble? And even if a mighty army surrounds me, my heart will not be afraid, for even when I am attacked, I will remain confident.

Teach me how to take enemy territory back for the Kingdom of God, little by little, and hold the ground. Teach me how to be a Kingdom warrior, having on the whole armor of God so that I will be able to stand against the tricks of the enemy. As a warrior of the most High God that I will overcome the enemy by the Blood of the Lamb, by the Word of God and by the Word of my testimony. So Lord bless me as I grow in skill using the weapons of warfare that are not carnal, but mighty through God to the pulling down of strongholds. Bless me that I might be a blessing to others as I declare that no weapon formed against me shall prosper.

I declare that I am a Kingdom warrior for the Most High God. In Jesus Name, Amen.

Warrior Lesson Two

KNOW YOUR ENEMY

How does the New American Concordance describe a warrior?

WARRIOR -- a noun

Definition: **Soldier, fighter, fighting man (or woman), GI, man-at-arms, serviceman, a man or woman engaged or experienced in warfare; broadly: a person engaged in some struggle or conflict.**

There are a number of elements that we are at war with. We have at least five enemies for believers.

Read the following scriptures.

1. The Devil (Gen. 3:15, 2 Cor. 2:11, Eph. 6:12, James 4:7, 1 Pet. 5:8, Rev. 12:17)

2. The Flesh (Rom. 7:23, 1 Cor. 9: 25-27, 2 Cor. 12:7, Gal. 5:17, 1 Pet. 2:11)

3. Enemies (Psalms 38:19, 56:2, 59:3)

4. The World (John 16:33, 1 John 2:14, 15)

5. Death (1Cor. 15:26, Heb. 2:14, 15)

Discuss the Famous Warrior- David

Samuel 17 (New International Version, ©2010)

David and Goliath

1 Now the Philistines gathered their forces for war and assembled at Sokoh in Judah. They pitched camp at Ephes Dammim, between Sokoh and Azekah. 2 Saul and the Israelites assembled and camped in the Valley of Elah and drew up their **battle line** to meet the Philistines. 3 The Philistines occupied one hill and the Israelites another, with the valley between them.

4 **A champion named Goliath**, who was from Gath, came out of the Philistine camp. His height was six cubits and a span.[a] 5 He had a bronze helmet on his head and wore a coat of scale armor of bronze weighing five thousand shekels[b]; 6 on his legs he wore bronze greaves, and a bronze javelin was slung on his back. 7 His spear shaft was like a weaver's rod, and its iron point weighed six hundred shekels.[c] His shield bearer went ahead of him.

8 Goliath stood and shouted to the ranks of Israel, "Why do you come out and line up for battle? Am I not a Philistine, and are you not the servants of Saul? Choose a man and have him come down to me. 9 If he is able to fight and kill me, we will

become your subjects; but if I overcome him and kill him, you will become our subjects and serve us." ¹⁰ Then the Philistine said, "This day I defy the armies of Israel! Give me a man and let us fight each other." ¹¹ On hearing the Philistine's words, **Saul and all the Israelites were dismayed and terrified.**

¹² Now David was the son of an Ephrathite named Jesse, who was from Bethlehem in Judah. Jesse had eight sons, and in Saul's time he was very old. ¹³ Jesse's three oldest sons had followed Saul to the war: The firstborn was Eliab; the second, Abinadab; and the third, Shammah. ¹⁴ **David was the youngest.** The three oldest followed Saul, ¹⁵ but David went back and forth from Saul to tend his father's sheep at Bethlehem.

¹⁶ **For forty days the Philistine came forward every morning and evening and took his stand. (A WEARING DOWN...TESTING)**

¹⁷ Now Jesse said to his son David, "Take this ephah[d] of roasted grain and these ten loaves of bread for your brothers and hurry to their camp. ¹⁸ Take along these ten cheeses to the commander of their unit. See how your brothers are and bring back some assurance[e] from them. ¹⁹ They are with Saul and all the men of Israel in the Valley of Elah, fighting against the Philistines."

²⁰ Early in the morning David left the flock in the care of a shepherd, loaded up and set out, as Jesse had directed. He reached the camp as the army was going out to its battle positions, **shouting the war cry**. ²¹ Israel and the Philistines were drawing up their lines facing each other. ²² David left his things with the keeper of supplies, ran to the battle lines and asked his brothers how they were. ²³ As he was talking with them, Goliath, the Philistine champion from Gath, stepped out from his lines and **shouted his usual defiance, and David heard it**. ²⁴ Whenever the Israelites saw the man, they all fled from him in great fear.

²⁵ Now the Israelites had been saying, "Do you see how this man keeps coming out? He comes out to defy Israel. The king will give great wealth to the man who kills him. He will also give him his daughter in marriage and will exempt his family from taxes in Israel." **(REWARDS FROM KING SAUL)**

²⁶ David asked the men standing near him, "What will be done for the man who kills this Philistine and **removes this disgrace** from Israel? Who is this **uncircumcised Philistine** that he should defy the armies of the living God?"

²⁷ They repeated to him what they had been saying and told him, "This is what will be done for the man who kills him."

²⁸ When Eliab, David's oldest brother, heard him speaking with the men, he burned with anger at him and asked, "Why have you come down here? And with whom did you leave those few sheep in the wilderness? I know how conceited you are and how wicked your heart is; you came down only to watch the battle."

²⁹ "Now what have I done?" said David. "Can't I even speak?" ³⁰ He then turned away to someone else and brought up the same matter, and the men answered him as before. ³¹ What David said was overheard and reported to Saul, and Saul sent for him.

³² David said to Saul, "Let no one lose heart on account of this Philistine; your servant will go and fight him."

³³ Saul replied, "You are not able to go out against this Philistine and fight him; you are only a young man, and he has been a **warrior from his youth.**" (key)

³⁴ But David said to Saul, "Your servant has been keeping his father's sheep. When a lion or a bear came and carried off a sheep from the flock, ³⁵ I went after it, struck it and rescued the sheep from its mouth. When it turned on me, I seized it by its hair, struck it and killed it. ³⁶ Your servant has killed both the lion and the bear; this uncircumcised Philistine will be like one of them, because he has defied the armies of the living God. ³⁷ The LORD who rescued me from the paw of the lion and the paw of the bear will rescue me from the hand of this Philistine." (**Lion, bear**)

Saul said to David, "Go, and the LORD be with you."

³⁸ Then Saul dressed David in his own tunic. He put a coat of armor on him and a bronze helmet on his head. ³⁹ David fastened on his sword over the tunic and tried walking around, because he was not used to them.

"I cannot go in these," he said to Saul, "because I am not used to them." So he took them off. ⁴⁰ **Then he took his staff in his hand, chose five smooth stones** from the stream, put them in the pouch of his shepherd's bag and, with his sling in his hand, approached the Philistine.

⁴¹ Meanwhile, the Philistine, with his shield bearer in front of him, kept coming closer to David. ⁴² He looked David over and saw that he was little more than a boy, glowing with health and handsome, and he despised him. ⁴³ He said to David, "Am I a dog, that you come at me with sticks?" **And the Philistine cursed David** by his gods. ⁴⁴ "Come here," he said, "and I'll give your flesh to the birds and the wild animals!"

⁴⁵ David said to the Philistine, "**You come against me with sword and spear and javelin, but I come against you in the name of the LORD Almighty, the God of the armies of Israel, whom you have defied. ⁴⁶ This day the LORD will deliver you into my hands, and I'll strike you down and cut off your head. This very day I will give the carcasses of the Philistine army to the birds and the wild animals, and the whole world will know that there is a God in Israel. ⁴⁷ All those gathered here will know that it is not by sword or spear that the LORD saves; for the battle is the LORD's, and he will give all of you into our hands.**" (Prophesied to the Enemy His Defeat)

⁴⁸ As the Philistine moved closer to attack him, David ran quickly toward the battle line to meet him. ⁴⁹ Reaching into his bag and taking out a stone, he slung it and struck the Philistine on the f**orehead**. The stone sank into his forehead, and he fell facedown on the ground.

⁵⁰ So David triumphed over the Philistine with a sling and a stone; without a sword in his hand he struck down the Philistine and killed him.

⁵¹ David ran and stood over him. He took hold of the Philistine's sword and drew it from the sheath. **After he killed him, he cut off his head with the sword.**

When the Philistines saw that their hero was dead, **they turned and ran**. ⁵² Then the men of Israel and Judah surged forward with a shout and pursued the Philistines to the entrance of Gath[f] and to the gates of Ekron. Their dead were strewn along the Shaaraim road to Gath and Ekron. ⁵³ When the Israelites returned from chasing the Philistines, they plundered their camp. (**Goliath, the Strongman**)

⁵⁴ David took the Philistine's head and brought it to Jerusalem; he put the Philistine's weapons in his own tent. (**Use the Devil's weapon on him**)

⁵⁵ As Saul watched David going out to meet the Philistine, he said to Abner, commander of the army, "Abner, whose son is that young man?"

Abner replied, "As surely as you live, Your Majesty, I don't know."

⁵⁶ The king said, "Find out whose son this young man is."

⁵⁷ As soon as David returned from killing the Philistine, Abner took him and brought him before Saul, with David still holding the Philistine's head.

⁵⁸ "Whose son are you, young man?" Saul asked him.

David said, "I am the son of your servant Jesse of Bethlehem."

DAVID KNEW HIS ENEMY BUT HE KNEW GOD EVEN BETTER

A Look at the Philistines

Origin of the Philistines

In the Bible, Genesis 10:13 lists the Philistines as being descended from Ham. The Bible contains roughly 250 references to the Philistines or Philistia, and repeatedly refers to them as "uncircumcised", just like the Hamitic peoples, such as Canaanites, which the Bible relates encountered the Israelites following the Exodus. (*See, e.g.,* 1 Samuel 17:26-36, 2 Samuel 1:20, Judges 14:3) It has been suggested that the Philistines formed part of the "Sea Peoples" who repeatedly attacked Egypt during the later Nineteenth.

A key to their dominance lay in their more advanced material culture. While the Israelites and Canaanites of the highlands still practiced Bronze Age skills, the Philistines had advanced to an Iron Age culture, making them nearly invincible on the battlefield. I Samuel 13:19-22 informs us: Now there was no blacksmith to be found throughout all the land of Israel, for the Philistines said, "Lest the Hebrews make swords or spears." But all the Israelites would go down to the Philistines to sharpen each man's plowshare, his mattock, his ax, and his sickle; and the charge for sharpening was a pim [two-thirds of a shekel, an exorbitant price] for the plowshares, the mattocks, the forks, and the axes, and to set the points of the goads. So it came about, on the day of battle, that there was neither sword nor spear found in the hand of any of the people who were with Saul and Jonathan. But they were found with Saul and Jonathan his son.

Saul could muster only two swords among six hundred men (see verse 15)! Evidently, most of his soldiers fought with axes, mattocks, ox goads, sickles, or sharpened sticks. Recall that Samson never used a normal weapon either, resorting to the jawbone of a donkey or his bare hands. The Philistine army, however, was fully outfitted with the advanced weaponry of the day:

So the Lord was with Judah. And they drove out the inhabitants of the mountains, but they could not drive out the inhabitants of the lowland [the Philistines and Canaanites there], because they had chariots of iron. (Judges 1:19)

[Goliath] had a bronze helmet on his head, and he was armed with a coat of mail. . . . And he had bronze greaves on his legs and a bronze javelin was between his shoulders. Now the staff of his spear was like a weaver's beam, and his iron spearhead weighed six hundred shekels; and a shield-bearer went before him. (I Samuel 17:5-7)

Later, the account mentions that Goliath also carried a sword (verse 51). David, of course, having refused Saul's armor and sword because he was untrained in them, carried only "his staff in his hand; . . . five smooth stones from the brook, and . . . his sling" (verse 40). David's severe disadvantage in arms was typical for an Israelite before the might of the Philistines.

GROUP WORK

1. What weapons did David possess? -Group 1

2. Name the warrior characteristics that David possessed. -Group 2

3. What are the qualities of a warrior coward? (King Saul) -Group3

4. What was Israel's disadvantages with the Philistine army? Group 4

5. What advantages did Goliath have?- Group 5

Study Your Enemy

Names and Characteristics for Satan

Study this list of some of the names and characteristics for Satan in the Bible. Satan plays many roles and by knowing them it will give us a better understanding to his method of operation. You must become a wise warrior but also rely on the Holy Spirit to lead and guide you.

Name	Reference	Definition
Abaddon	Revelation 9:11	a destroying angel
The accuser of our brethren	Revelation 12:10	against one in the assembly, i.e. a complaintant at law; specially, Satan
The adversary	I Peter 5:8	an opponent (in a lawsuit); specially, Satan (as the arch-enemy)
Apollyon	Revelation 9:11	a destroyer (i.e. Satan)
Beelzebub	Matthew 12:24 Mark 3:22 Luke 11:15	dung-god; Beelzebul, a name of Satan
Belial	II Corinthians 6:15	worthlessness; Belial, as an epithet of Satan
the Devil	Matthew 4:1	a traducer; specially, Satan: false accuser, devil, slanderer.
Dragon	Revelation 12:9 and 20:2	probably from an alternate form of derkomai (to look); a fabulous kind of serpent (perhaps as supposed to fascinate)
Name	Reference	Definition
the enemy	Matthew 13:39	from a primary echtho (to hate); hateful (passively, odious, or actively, hostile); usually as a noun, an adversary (especially Satan)
father of all l	John 8:44	a falsifier, lies
Name	Reference	Definition
king of Babylon	Isaiah 14:4	confusion; Babel (i.e. Babylon), including Babylonia and the Babylonian empire
king of Tyrus	Ezekiel 28:12	a rock; Tsor, a place in Palestine. Satan is the false rock. Christ is the true Rock.
little horn	Daniel 7:8	a horn (as projecting); by implication, a flask, cornet; by resembl. an elephant's tooth (i.e. ivory), a corner (of the

		altar), a peak (of a mountain), a ray (of light); figuratively, power
Lucifer	Isaiah 14:12	(in the sense of brightness); the morning star: lucifer (the king of Babylon). Satan is the false morning star. Christ is the true morning Star.
man of sin	II Thessalonians 2:3	Satan was the first to sin. See Ezekiel 28:11-19
that old serpent	Revelation 12:9 and 20:2	old = original or primeval serpent = (through the idea of sharpness of vision); a snake, figuratively (as a type of sly cunning) an artful malicious person, especially Satan
power of darkness	Colossians 1:13	"shade" or a shadow (literally or figuratively [darkness of error or an adumbration])
prince of the power of the air	Ephesians 2:2	prince = a first (in rank or power) power = privilege, i.e. (subjectively) force, capacity, competency, freedom, or (objectively) mastery (concretely, magistrate, superhuman, potentate, token of control), delegated influence
prince that shall come	Daniel 9:26	a commander (as occupying the front), civil, military or religious; generally (abstractly, plural), honorable themes. See II Thessalonians 2:3-4 and Revelation 12:7-9
prince of Tyrus	Ezekiel 28:2	a rock; Tsor, a place in Palestine. Satan is the false rock. Christ is the true Rock.
prince of this world	John 12:31	prince = a first (in rank or power) world = orderly arrangement, i.e. decoration; by implication, the world (in a wide or narrow sense, including its inhabitants, literally or figuratively [morally])
rulers of the darkness of this world	Ephesians 6:12	rulers = a world-ruler, an epithet of Satan darkness = shadiness, i.e. obscurity (literally or figuratively)
Satan	Job 1:6	an opponent; especially (with the article prefixed) Satan, the arch-enemy of good.
Name	**Reference**	**Definition**
Serpent	Genesis 3:1	properly, to hiss, i.e. whisper a (magic) spell; generally, to prognosticate
son of perdition	John 17:12 II Thessalonians 2:3	ruin or loss (physical, spiritual or eternal) also to destroy fully (reflexively, to perish, or lose), literally or figuratively

the tempter	Matthew 4:3	to test (objectively), i.e. endeavor, scrutinize, entice, discipline
the wicked one	Matthew 13:19	hurtful, i.e. evil (properly, in effect or influence) figuratively, calamitous; also (passively) ill, i.e. diseased; but especially (morally) culpable, i.e. derelict, vicious, facinorous; neuter (singular) mischief, malice, or (plural) guilt; masculine (singular) the devil, or (plural) sinners

Homework: Study the names and attributes of the enemy

WEEK THREE--Five Minute Review Quiz

Match the names of Satan to the scripture passage.

1. ____ serpent
2. ____ king of Babylon
3. ____ prince of the power of the air
4. ____ prince of Tyrus
5. ____ Lucifer
6. ____ son of perdition
7. ____ the tempter
8. ____ the wicked one
9. ____ little horn
10. ____ the adversary
11. ____ Abaddon
12. ____ Accuser of the Brethren
13. ____ Beelzebub
14. ____ Dragon
15. ____ father of lies
16. ____ Satan
17. ____ Belial

a. Revelation 9:11
b. Revelation 12:10
c. I Peter 5:8
d. Matthew 12:24
e. II Corinthians 6:15
f. Revelation 12:9
g. John 8:44
h. Isaiah 14:4
i. Ezekiel 28:2
j. Isaiah 14:12
l. Job 1:6
m. Genesis 3:1
n. John 17:12
o. Daniel 7:8
p. Matthew 13:19
q. Ephesians 2:2
r. Matthew 4:3

WARRIOR LESSON 3

Satan's Harassment Plan and

HOW TO TORMENT THE DEVIL

Our Lord and Savior understands what it's like to be tortured and tormented by the Devil. He knew how to master the Devil's plans and confront Him with the Word of God. The Lord Jesus knew Satan's tactics inside and out. He was not overtaken or overwhelmed by the enemy.

Matthew 4:5-11 (King James Version)

⁵Then the devil taketh him up into the holy city, and setteth him on a pinnacle of the temple,

⁶And saith unto him, If thou be the Son of God, cast thyself down: for it is written, He shall give his angels charge concerning thee: and in their hands they shall bear thee up, lest at any time thou dash thy foot against a stone.

⁷Jesus said unto him, It is written again, Thou shalt not tempt the Lord thy God.

⁸Again, the devil taketh him up into an exceeding high mountain, and sheweth him all the kingdoms of the world, and the glory of them;

⁹And saith unto him, All these things will I give thee, if thou wilt fall down and worship me.

¹⁰Then saith Jesus unto him, Get thee hence, Satan: for it is written, Thou shalt worship the Lord thy God, and him only shalt thou serve.

¹¹Then the devil leaveth him, and, behold, angels came and ministered unto him.

When the Enemy tortures and torments a believer, it means they have something valuable the enemy wants to destroy. What do you have that the enemy wants to destroy?

Write your answer here:

_____

_____

_____

WARRIORS FOR CHRIST NEED TRAINING IN SPIRITUAL TERROSIM.

A LOOK AT TERRORISM IN THE BIBLE

1. Satan, is **the first Terrorist** and the father of Terrorism TODAY. HE made his appearance in the Garden of Eden and struck up a conversation with Eve. She did not know she was talking to a Suicide bomber. She didn't have any experience with terrorism. But it was the serpent's hatred for God's creation that sent him on a mission of destruction that day in the Garden. Adam and Eve terrorist attack was not just about them, but all mankind. The roots of terrorism entered the earth, **through sin, hatred, fear and death. The root of all terrorism is HATRED.**

2. **J**oseph met his first terrorist right in his own family. His brothers rose up against him and tried to kill him. It seemed that he was always in a terrorist situation, but God raised him up from prison to the palace, and his terrorists had to bow in the end.

3. **"According to the Bible, Moses and Aaron organized the first Israelite army when leaving Egyptian bondage. (page 37- Battles of the Bible)"** Moses met his terrorist called **Pharaoh, and** Pharaoh had a mighty army, but Moses defeated Pharaoh in the Name of the Lord. The Red Sea was opened and Pharaoh's army was drowned as Moses learned how to "stand still" and see the salvation of the Lord in the midst of a terrorist attack.

4. **David met** Goliath and Goliath was a terrorist. Goliath was talking trash and all of Israel was afraid. Fear struck in the heart even of King Saul.

But David brought Goliath down in the Name of the Lord of Host with a little sling and a stone, like a young Navy Seal in the Spirit.

5. **Saul, who later became Apostle Paul had a** unique story, for he was first a terrorist himself, killing Christians and dragging them out of their houses. He was a religious terrorist justifying his blood acts through religion. But God had a Damascus Road experience for him. Then Saul, became Paul and many in the Church didn't trust him and still tried to kill him. There is still some terrorist activity in the Church today. They are religious and they don't like anybody that is different from them. They want to bomb in the Spirit anything new and fresh that God wants to do. Saul understands terrorism for he had lived on both sides of it.

If Satan is bothering you, or if he is threatening you, it is only because you have something valuable on the inside of you that he wants to destroy. Do you know what that treasure is on the inside of you? Once you find out who you are and what God has put on the inside of you, the enemy is gonna test you, and torture you, and torment you. Remember that greater One is on the inside of you than He that is in the world. **It's time for the saints to torment the Devil!** It's time for the warriors to tread upon him. It's time for us to be the head and not the tail.

Does this Torture Plan look familiar to you? Every Believer, warrior, intercessor and church leader needs *"torture training"* in the Spirit. We must take heed to the Word that declares. (John `10:10)

Either you are going to let the Devil torture and torment you or you are going to rise up and torment the Devil! You are going to be most miserable in this life if you don't get some training in overcoming the devil's harassment programs. YOU ARE NOT EXEMPT FROM TORTURE BY THE ENEMY. HE HATES THE CHILDREN OF GOD!

What is the purpose of torture?

- Torture, which uses physical or moral violence to extract confessions, punish the guilty, frighten opponents, or satisfy hatred is contrary to respect for the person and for human dignity.
-

Why Does Satan like to torture believers?

- **1. He wants to satisfy his hatred. He Hates God and hates God's children**

- **2. He wants to extract a confession that will damage God and the Kingdom of God**

- **3. He is a terrorist, murderer, liar and a thief.**

- **4. He wants to punish God's children without a cause**

- **5. He wants to frighten and intimidate his opponents**

- **6. He wants to brainwash the saints with lies**

- **7. He knows his time is short and his expected end in the Lake of Fire where he will be tortured forever and ever in the Lake of Fire.**

ABC's of Satan's Torture Plan

Discuss this comprehensive list of how the Devil tortures believers and warriors. We must be ready for his attacks.

Circle the tactics Satan uses on you.

A- Accusation, anxiety, addiction, aging, abuse, angel of light, absence of peace, anger, allergies, abandonment, accidents, abortion, adultery, alcoholism, anguish, asthma, apathy, arthritis, arguments, atheism, anti-christ spirits, ADHD, alzheimers, AIDS/HIV

B- Brainwashing, buffet you, blocking spirits, backsliding, bewitchment, backlash, bondage, bitterness, bombardment, blood covenants, backbiting, barrenness, betrayal, burdens

C- Condemnation, curses, crying, control, confusion, chaos, cruelty, cyphone, chronic illness ,cults

D- Demons, death, disease, depression, deception, doctrines of demons, delusion, discord, destruction, division, doubt, dread, darkness, divorce, domination

E- Exhaustion, embarrassment, emptiness, emotional rollercoaster, escape

F- Frustration, financial disaster, fatherlessness, fatigue, fear, failure, front lash, forgetfulness, false teaching, false religions, false gods, fornication, fear of hell, feces, familiar spirits, fighting, filth, fortune telling, freemasonry

G- Guilt, grief, gluttony, greed, generational curses, gossip, gambling, gloom, guile

H- Harassment, hunter of souls, humiliation, hatred, horror, hell, hurt, deep hurt, hallucinations, homosexuality, hardships, headstrong, hypocrisy

I- Infirmity, isolation, insomnia, infiltration, interference, injecting thoughts/feelings, ignorance, insanity, interrogation, idolatry, immorality, insanity, insecurity, infections

J- Jezebel, jealousy

K-Knifelike pains in the heart, Korah spirits

L-Lack, laziness, legion, leviathan, lethargy, lust, lying, lesser demons, low self esteem, legalism

M-Mammon, magick, manipulation, martial arts, masturbation, me3dication, melancholy, mental illness, mind blinding, mind control, misery, mockery, molestation, murder, magnification, mayhem, misunderstanding

N-Nightmares, night attacks, nausea, necromancy, nervousness

O-Occult, offence, opposition, overwhelmed, oppression, obstruction, octopus, obscenity, outcast

P-PAIN, poverty, palmistry, perfectionism, paranoia, passivity, psychological warfare, pressure, punishment, paralysis, panic attacks, pride, profanity, pharmekia, power of demonic suggestion, the past, persecution, perversion, phobias, pornography, python, prejudice, psychic, prostitution, promiscuity

Q-Quick tempered

R-Ruler demons, rage, rejection, resentment, religious spirits, racism, restless, rape, rebellion, relapse, resistance, retardation, retaliation, revenge, rigid, rude

S-Suicide, sleep deprivation, shame, self pity, suffering, sadistic, slander, secrets, slumber, slavery, Satanism, stubborn spirits, schizophrenia, scorpion, séance, seduction, selfishness, serpent power, sickness, siege warfare, slander, slothful, soothsaying, sorcery, sorrow, soul ties, spiritism, spite, sealing, stiff necked, stress, superstition

T-Threatening, trespassing, torment, temptation, timidity, trauma, tricks, taskmaster, temper, third eye, tragedy, trouble, tumors

U-Unbelief, unforgiveness, unaware, urine, uncleanliness, unworthy, unteachableness

V-Vicious Cycles, violence, vain imaginations, vomit, vagabond, vanity, victimization, voodoo, vampirism, vexation, vision thieves, vulgar

W-Warlock, whoredoms, witchcraft, weariness, wounded spirit, wickedness, worry, withdrawal, worldliness, warfare, wager, weakness, wizards, witch covens, wrestling

X- X-rated

Y-Yoga

Z-Zeal without knowledge

Homework

READ ALOUD IN CLASS AND AT HOME THIS WEEK

40 Ways TO TORMENT AND TORTURE THE DEVIL (ENEMY)

1. Forbid demons to speak or communicate
2. Cast demons out and command demons to exit and go
3. Ask God to let His Angels chase the demons
4. Pray with your understanding and in your prayer language (Tongues)
5. Read the Word of God out loud
6. Speak, sing, and pray in the Name of Jesus
7. Apply and appropriate the Blood of Jesus
8. Preach the Kingdom of God
9. Bind and rebuke demons and loose the will of God
10. Release the love of Jesus Christ where there is demonic activity and darkness
11. Call for angelic help and assistance
12. Fast and pray
13. Worship the Lord in Spirit and in truth
14. Prophesy and declare the Word of the Lord
15. Walk in unity as the people of God
16. Flow in the Word of Wisdom
17. Flow in the Word of Knowledge
18. Flow in the discerning of spirits
19. Submit to the Lord and resist Satan and he will have to flee
20. Be a covenant keeper

21. Confess your sins and live a life of repentance
22. Obey the Lord and keep His commandments
23. Seek the Kingdom of God first and His righteousness
24. Keep the greatest commandments (Love God, Love one another)
25. Be quick to forgive, slow to speak and slow to get angry
26. Flow in revelation knowledge from the Lord
27. Work in teams and not alone when dealing with the enemy
28. Humble yourself before the Lord
29. Be filled with Spirit of God
30. Renew your mind daily in the Word of God
31. Study the Word of God to show yourself approved of God
32. Have the assurance of your salvation
33. Witness and tell others about Jesus Christ everywhere you go
34. Love not your life unto death, but lay your life down for the Kingdom
35. In everything give thanks and have joy
36. Keep on the whole armor of God
37. Remind Satan of his end (Rev. 20:10)
38. Sing songs about the Blood of Jesus (Blood songs)
39. Walk by faith and not by sight
40. Sow into the Kingdom of God (tithes, time, talents)

WEEK FOUR--Five Minute Review Quiz

List ten biblical ways you torment the Devil.

1.

2.

3.

4.

5.

6.

7.

8.

9.

10.

What is it on the "inside of you" that the Devil hates and is trying to "kill, steal and destroy" from you?

_____

_____

_____

WARRIOR LESSON 4

How to Fight an Invisible Enemy

As God's warriors, we recognize that we are not fighting against flesh and blood or against each other, but against an enemy that we are not evenly matched with. We are already at a disadvantage with Satan if we try to fight him in our human strength and human intellect. **We are no match for the Devil.** This is the first bit of wisdom that you must learn in Warriors 101. Hear the words of a song by Martin Luther as he describes this ancient foe. Discuss the Word of this old hymn. What do we learn about our ancient, invisible foe and about our GOD?

A MIGHTY FORTRESS IS OUR GOD

(Music and Words by Martin Luther)

A mighty fortress is our God, a bulwark never failing;
Our helper He, amid the flood of mortal ills prevailing:
For still our ancient foe doth seek to work us woe;
His craft and power are great, and, armed with cruel hate,
On earth is not his equal.

Did we in our own strength confide, our striving would be losing;
Were not the right Man on our side, the Man of God's own choosing:
Dost ask who that may be? Christ Jesus, it is He;
Lord Sabaoth, His Name, from age to age the same,
And He must win the battle.

And though this world, with devils filled, should threaten to undo us,
We will not fear, for God hath willed His truth to triumph through us:
The Prince of Darkness grim, we tremble not for him;
His rage we can endure, for lo, his doom is sure,
One little word shall fell him.

That word above all earthly powers, no thanks to them, abideth;
The Spirit and the gifts are ours through Him Who with us sideth:
Let goods and kindred go, this mortal life also;
The body they may kill: God's truth abideth still,
His kingdom is forever.

"While we look not at the things which are seen, but at the things which are not seen, for the things which are seen are temporal; but the things which are not seen are eternal." 2nd Corinthians 4:18.

Ephesians 6 states :

"11 Put on the whole armor of God, that you may be able to stand against the wiles of the devil. 12 For we do not wrestle against flesh and blood, but against principalities, against powers, against the rulers of the darkness of this age, against spiritual hosts of wickedness in the heavenly places. 13 Therefore take up the whole armor of God, that you may be able to withstand in the evil day, and having done all, to stand."

How Does a Christian Battle these Invisible Enemies?

12 Key Principles

1. Just because you don't see Satan's kingdom, doesn't mean it does not exist.

2. Satan's greatest weapon is making believers think he does not exist.

3. We must be spiritually mature to deal with the invisible enemy and we must have spiritual eyes to see.

4. Our discernment and discerning of spirits is key in being as warrior for God.

5. We are not match for this "ancient foe." Therefore we must stay under the blood covering of Jesus Christ and the wisdom of God to fight this unseen world.

6. We must not open ourselves up to "forbidden realms" of the occult.

7. We must not spend more time hunting for the Devil and occult secrets or realms than we spend worshipping the Lord and studying His Word. We must keep ourselves in a place of obedience and holiness in order to be the kind of warrior God can use.

8. We can see the effects of Satan's kingdom through the works of darkness in the world today. We must discern first want is manifesting in the natural realm to discern the invisible realms. Some believers are blind to the things they can see around them everyday. The natural realm that we can see ***reveals clearly the things planned and going on in the invisible realms.***

9. "One command given to believers dealing with Satan is to resist the devil. James 4:7 tells us that we are to submit ourselves to God and resist the devil and he will flee from us. We are given much better weapons to fight Satan and the demonic forces: "we must be delivered from the power of the evil one by believing, praying, repenting, obeying, seeking, and serving.

10. Putting on the armour of God. Ephesians 6:10–20 tell us that we are to resist the work of Satan and his demons by arming ourselves. The focus is obedient living. "Biblical spiritual warfare is not about knowing Satan—it is about so knowing God and walking with Him that we readily recognize the counterfeit offers of the Enemy. Putting on the armor is about making disciples through teaching…. his point was that faithful Christian living is itself effective in undermining the Enemy."Lawless offers a holistic approach to spiritual warfare through right living and obedience to God. Spiritual warfare is won through the exaltation of God through worship, evangelizing the world, equipping believers, edifying others, encountering God through prayer and the Word, and encouraging one another.

11. Success in battle is living obedient and holy lives to God the Father through the provision of the Son, and the power of the Spirit. God has not told us how to detect demons, how to know their names, or how to cast them out. Instead, He has exhorted us repeatedly in His Word to shun sin, make no place for Satan in our lives, and resist the devil by obeying the Lord. At the moment of salvation Jesus delivers the believing one form the power of darkness and transfers him or her into the kingdom of God's dear Son (Col. 1:14). We need to put into practice the victory Christ has already achieved for us, always keeping in mind the exalted position we have in Him. Satan is a defeated foe. Victory is ours in Christ and Him alone.

12. Satan hates the Blood of Jesus Christ. This is a major weapon against the hosts of Hell and it provides a covering for us that our human minds cannot explain. The Devil hates the Name of Jesus of Christ and the Word of God. These three fold cords of The Blood, The Name and The Word never fail and never lose it's power. (Rev. 12:10-11)

25 Ways to Fight and Win Against the (Invisible)Unseen World

© 2008 by Dr. Jackie L. Green (Watchdog Training Manual)

Circle the areas that you need to grow up in and use more frequently, in order to be a stronger warrior for the Lord.

1. Resist the Enemy – James 4:7
2. Pulling Down Strongholds- II Corinthians 10:3-5
3. Prayer and Fasting- Isaiah 58:5-8
4. Prophesy- Ezekiel 37:1-10
5. Preach the Word- I Timothy 4:2
6. Fire of the Lord- II Kings 18:36-40
7. The Blood of Jesus Christ – Revelation 12:10
8. The Word of Your Testimony- Revelation 12:10
9. No Fear of Death- Revelation 12:10
10. The Name of Jesus Christ- Proverbs 18:10, Psalms 124:8
11. The Full Armor of God- Ephesians 6:10-18
12. Decree and Declare- Job 22:28 and Psalms 2:-8
13. Righteousness (Righteous living) James 5:16 and Isaiah 11:5
14. Casting out devils- Matthew 10:1
15. The Keys of the Kingdom- (Binding and Loosing) Matthew 16:19
16. The Lord's Supper (power of communion and unity) I Corinthians 11:23-25
17. Kingdom Authority (power of the Spirit) I Corinthians 4:20
18. Faith- Hebrews 11:33
19. Power to Bless and love our enemies- I Corinthians 4:12
20. Our Voice- (TRUMPET) Isaiah 58:1, Mark 1:3, Psalms 26:7, Ezekiel 33:3-6

DISCUSS THE SEEN AND UNSEEN REALMS

Which areas are forbidden for warriors to encounter?

Read: Revelation 20:14, Revelation 20:3, II Peter 2:4 and Jude 6, Luke 23:43 and Matthew 16:18

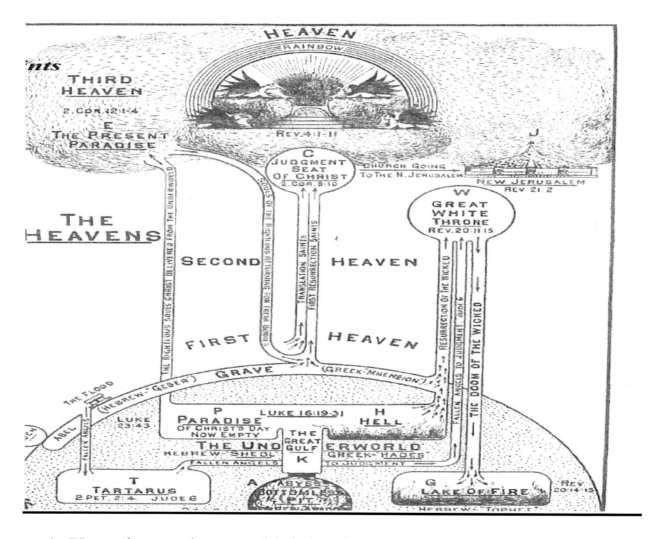

1. How do you know which battles to fight?
2. How do you get your battle instructions?
3. Are there "forbidden realms" we are not to touch?

For Homework Study the Warrior Scriptures in the Appendix.

WEEK FIVE - Five Minute Review Quiz

The Whole Armor of God.

List the Whole Amor of God and what each piece is used for.

1.

2.

3.

4.

5.

6.

7.

What are the five compartments of the underworld?

1. _____ Revelation 20:14

2 _____ Revelation 20:3

3. _____ II Peter 2:4 and Jude 6

4. _____ Luke 23:43

5. _____ Matthew 16:18

WARRIOR LESSON 5

Joshua, The Conquering Warrior

A Look atThree Battles

"The great problem for the Israelites, who were inexperienced in siege craft and devoid of any siege training, was of course, the capture of the town, secured as it was behind it's walls, towers and battlements. Joshua therefore commanded his scouts to reconnoiter the other side of the Jordon for the best possible bridge head, with special emphasis upon Jericho, and their exploits are common knowledge.

Battle One- Jericho- God Uses Strange Battle Strategies

Joshua 6:1-5 (New International Version, ©2011)

Joshua 6

¹ Now the gates of Jericho were securely barred because of the Israelites. No one went out and no one came in.

² Then the LORD said to Joshua, "See, I have delivered Jericho into your hands, along with its king and its fighting men. ³ March around the city once with all the armed men. Do this for six days. ⁴ Have seven priests carry trumpets of rams' horns in front of the ark. On the seventh day, march around the city seven times, with the priests blowing the trumpets. ⁵ When you hear them sound a long blast on the trumpets, have the whole army give a loud shout; then the wall of the city will collapse and the army will go up, everyone straight in."

JOSHUA CHAPTER SIX- THE BATTLE OF JERICHO

Commentary Notes...

1	Jericho was an important city. It had an abundant spring and the people could grow crops year round. It was an oasis in the desert with the nickname "City of Palms." It was near a ford in the Jordan River (passable except during the spring flooding), and was on the east-west trade route to Jerusalem. It was a strategic place both in military and political terms. The walls around Jericho are thought to have been about 45 feet high. The walls were thick and sloped to resist siege tactics such as ladders and battering rams.
2	In God's eyes, the victory was already won. It was just a matter of time until Joshua would live that victory. The enemy's fear was promised by God and was evidence that He would fulfil His promise to give the Israelites victory. This would be a big victory because Jericho was well fortified, had its own king, and had valiant warriors. The Israelites were not trained warriors, but God would be their warrior.
3	The next week would be a week of increasing dread for the people of Jericho. If the city (or individuals) had surrendered, God would have had mercy on them. This idea is compatible with God's character, but we will see that no one surrenders, keeping with God's assessment of their spiritual hopelessness. Rehab had already surrendered, so God and Israel would provide protection for her.
4	Again, the ark is the symbol of the presence of God. The priests were to announce the approach of God with the sounding of ram's horn trumpets (*shophar*). There are other places when God's presence is announced with the sounding of a trumpet (Exo 19:16, Rev 11:15). Trumpets were occasionally used as musical instruments, but were most commonly used as signaling instruments. Trumpets were also used in other places to aid in directing troops in battle, or to celebrate religious festivals.
	.
5	Large armies have a rear guard to make sure that the army is not defeated by a surprise attack from behind. This does not diminish the significance pointed out in verse seven because there is another point of symbolism here: God is the center and the focal point of the army.

6	The army was absolutely silent. They were not to shout prematurely. They were not to give a war cry or even taunt the people inside the city. It was like a funeral procession for the city, announcing its impending destruction. This certainly unnerved the city people even more than they had been before.
7	The Bible does not tell us how long it took to circle the city. However, it is believed that the city covered ten acres, which might have taken half an hour to an hour to circumnavigate.
8	In order to accomplish everything that day, Israel had to rise early. Certainly, an army of about 530,000 men terrified the people (Num 1, Josh 4:12-13). The army of Israel may have stretched out long enough to surround the city as they marched. To have this massive army march around the city seven times would have magnified their anxiety.
9	The city had been marked for complete destruction. The unrepentant pagans of the city were to be executed according to God's judgment.
10	The Israelites were not to take any plunder from this battle. In future battles they would share in the spoils of battle, but for now, they were not. This is to emphasize that the battle was not won by men, but by God.
11	Every perishable thing (those that would not survive fire) were to be destroyed along with the city. Metals, however, could be purified by fire, and thus be dedicated to God.
12	Every person was killed in accordance with God's judgment against them. Every animal was to be killed because either they were considered defiled, or they were dedicated to God to commemorate this first victory in the Promised Land.
13	Since the spies had made the promise, Joshua sends them to fulfill it. Rahab would recognize and trust them.
14	Everything that was perishable was burned. Everything that could pass through the fire was set apart for God. God's treasury would serve to remind Israel of the great victories He gave them. It would also be a source of funding for the upkeep of the tabernacle (and later the temple) as well as the priests.
15	At first, Rahab and her family were placed outside the camp. Everything "unclean" was to be placed outside the camp. Indeed, fresh from their pagan

	surroundings, this family was considered unclean. Later, however, they became part of Israel. Rahab eventually married an Israelite named Salmon and their son Boaz was the great grandfather of King David (Mat 1:5-6).
16	God had marked Jericho for destruction. The city would be rebuilt, but the man who would be in charge of the reconstruction would be cursed for his arrogance. This prophesy is fulfilled in 1 Ki 16:34. Even so, Jericho is not beyond redemption. Jesus in His day would visit Jericho and find people of faith (Luke 18:35-19:10).
17	Joshua not only gained the respect of the Israelites, but of the surrounding nations as well. This miraculous victory would continue to destroy the moral of the armies of the land. They would sense that their doom was certain. Although many would fight against Israel, their feared destruction would happen.

GOD CAN TEACH US MUCH ABOUT WARFARE

1. The enemy that we are fighting is not flesh and blood.
2. The great problem for the Israelites is that they were inexperienced in siege craft warfare and any siege warfare training to capture a town.
3. As believers, sometimes we don't want to do any research or scouting out before we jump into warfare. We need to do our research, our homework, our prayer and fasting and consulting the Lord before every battle.
4. Joshua's used the strategy of "fooling the enemy" and giving the enemy a sense of false security.
5. Joshua utilized "midnight hours."
6. In ancient military strategies, you had to consider the army size, unit type, terrain, weather, positional advantage, skill level and individual battle experience. Since Israel lacked in battle experience, God gave them instructions and He won the battle.

Battle Two- AI

1. Ai had been a heavily fortified town 1300 years before Joshua's time. The scouts went out to evaluate the battle, but thought it was a piece of cake. They were over-confident by repeated success.
2. The fall or defeat of Israel at Ai shook the Israelites. What were the reasons they lost the battle:

    1. Over-confidence
    2. Did not consult the Lord over man
    3. Sin the Camp
    4. Gathering "intelligence" information may not always be reliable.
    5. Unfamiliar with their enemy
    6. Underestimated the enemy forces

BATTLE THREE- AI BATTLE RESTAGED
JOSHUA 11

1. Joshua immediately deals with sin in the camp.
2. Joshua decides to crush his enemy immediately before dawn.
3. Joshua prayed and God gave him an "ambush stragegy." He caught them off guard before they could deploy on more open ground.
4. Joshua was fully aware of his limitations.

5. Joshua won battles in the Lord along with Israelites qualities of speed, stealth and knowledge of the terrain and crushed the unbeatable enemy.

WHAT WARRIOR PRINCIPLES DO WE LEARN FROM JOSHUA'S GIBBEONITE EXPERIENCE?

JOSHUA CHAPTER 9

Gibbeonite Relationships

A Gibbeonite Relationship is sent by Satan in times when we are at a crossroad and making major decisions that could crush him. Any relationships that we connect with without consulting God first has the potential to destroy us or bind us. Gibbeonites are deceptive relationships with a hidden agenda.)
Remember: Relationships are so important to God that He sent His Son to die on the cross that our relationship with God could be restored. We have had fallen relationships since the Adam and Eve fell in the Garden. Relationships are invisible covenants we make that have public results. Some relationships are (l) Kairos (2) Long Term (3) Short Term (4) Life Long (5) Markers only

Relationship Battles – The Gibbeonites

Always Consult God before you Fight a Battle

"Every relationship will move you closer to God and purpose or draw you away from God and purpose."

Many of life's battles is with relationships. Share the type of relationship and the type of battle you have had in relationship.

Relationship   **Type of Battle**

1. _____

2. _____

3. _____

4. _____

We can learn a great lesson from King David's life and his experiences in a tough relationship with King Saul.

Read: *"Saul-Jonathan-David Relationships"- I Samuel 18:1-16*

Key Verse: "And David behaved wisely in all his ways, and the Lord was with him." I Samuel 18:14

God wants us to form relationships with those who have

(1) First and foremost a heart after God
(2) Those who will not compromise
(3) Those who fear God more than they fear man
(4) Those who can forgive when they have been attacked by Saul. David was attacked by Saul all his life- 21 times but never touched Saul.
(5) Be in a relationship with those who are not jealous of you and know who they are in Christ.
(6) Not dependent on people encouraging you, for David had to learn to encourage himself
(7) Be in relationship with those who do not backbite, gossip and speak against those in authority.
(8) Form relationships with those who know who you are and respect that (David was the King even through Saul was on the throne)
(9) Be Mindful of those that want to control the anointing on your life
(10) When you come into power and authority over the lives of others, do not become like Saul.
(11) When you have to be in relationship with those who are ungodly or carnal or an adversary to you, you must be the one with integrity and righteousness and be a good witness even if it hurts.
(12) When you are in relationships because of bloodline/family, and you are forced to be around them from time to time, recognize that God wants us to treat all people fairly and with respect, but we don't have to become like them. We can be in the world, or even in the "family" but not of the world or like the family we have come out of.

WEEK SIX- Five Minute Review Quiz

TRUE OR FALSE- Battles of Joshua

1. ____ The greatest problem for the Israelites was that they were inexperienced in siege craft warfare and siege training.
2. ____ When Israel took the ark of the covenant into battle, it was a symbol of God's presence.
3. ____ When Joshua and the Israelites followed God's instructions the City of Jericho still did not fear them.
4. ____ When the walls of Jericho fell down flat, the Israelites could have the whole city, move in and live there.
5. ____ In Jericho, God instructed them once the city was destroyed to also destroy the gold, silver and brass.
6. ____ Rahab helped to hide the spies that Joshua sent in. She was a priest of Jericho.
7. ____ Once Jericho was brought down, Joshua decided to reward anyone that rebuilt the city of Jericho.
8. ____ The surrounding cities had heard about the victory of Joshua and the Israelites and they feared the same destruction would happen to them.
9. ____ Joshua fought the battle and AI and lost because he was sick and in bed.
10. ____ Israel lost the battle to AI because they were overconfident, had sin in the camp and underestimated the enemy.
11. ____ Achan was among the Israelite camp that had brought a curse upon the Israelites because he had stolen and hid something the plunder from Jericho (silver coines, a beautiful robe and a bar of gold) and buried it beneath his tent.
12. ____ Joshua and the leaders of Israel forgave Achan for the trouble he brought on Israel.
13. ____ Joshua and the Israelites stoned Achan and his family and burned their bodies and named the place Valley of Trouble to this day.
14. ____ Joshua and the Isaelites did go and defeat AI the second time with 30,000 of their best warriors. The Lord renewed His covenant with them and Joshua built an altar.
15. ____ When the people of Gibeon heard what Joshua had done to Jericho and AI, they resorted to deception to save themselves.
16. ____ Joshua and the Israelites were deceived by the Gibbeonites because they did not consult the Lord first and made a peace treaty with them.
17. ____ Three months after making the peace treaty Joshua and the Israelites found out the Gibeonites tricked them and lived nearby.
18. ____ Because the Gibbeonties tricked Joshua and the Israelites, Joshua did not allow the people of Israel to kill them but made the Gibeonites the woodcutters and water carriers for the community and for the altar of the Lord.
19. ____ All of our relationships either draw us closer to our purpose or draws us away from purpose and destiny.
20. ____ Joshua used "night warfare" to crush and ambush AI.

WARRIOR LESSON 6

Night Warriors- Night Warfare

"The church, God's warriors and new works or ministries have lost a lot of battles because they only wanted to fight in the daytime, on their terms and when it was convenient."

(Bishop Jackie Green)

Jesus Christ our Lord is the greatest example of a night warrior. Here in Luke 22, we find the account of Jesus praying into the night, but His disciples could not stay awake.

Luke 22:39 -46 (New Living Translation)

39 Then, accompanied by the disciples, Jesus left the upstairs rooman and went as usual to the Mount to of Olives. **40** There he told them, "*Pray that you will not give in to temptation.*" **41** He walked away, about a stone's throw, and knelt down and prayed. **42** *"Father, if you are willing, please take this cup of suffering away from me."* **43** Then an angel from heaven appeared and strengthened him. **44** He prayed more fervently, and he was in such agony of spirit that his sweat fell to the ground like great drops of blood. **45** At last he stood up again and returned to the disciples, only to find them asleep, exhausted from grief. **46** *"Why are you sleeping?* He asked them. *"Get up and pray, so that you will not given into temptation."*

Seven key principles for night warfare from our Lord in this text:

We must be alert to:

1. *Fatigue/exhaustion-* Verse - _____
2. *Heavy Slumber spirits-* Verse - _____
3. *Weakness/Seduction spirits-* Verse_____
4. *Agony (Suffering /mental torment)* Verse _____
5. *Realizing we need angelic help-* Verse_____
6. *Grief/divided emotions -* Verse _____
7. *Have a consecrated place to pray-* Verse_____

Night Warfare Worksheet

A Forgotten Strategy in the Body of Christ

Read the scripture and fill in the following night warfare chart below.

Text	Warrior	Enemy	Strategy
Genesis 14:15-16	Abraham	Kedorlaomer's Army	Mobilized 318 men at night/recovered all
Exodus 12:12, 31-42			
Exodus 14:21-25			
Joshua 8:13-20			
Judges 16:1-6			
I Samuel 31:11-13			
II Kings 19:35			
Nehemiah 2:12-15, 4:9			

26 Qualification for Night Warriors

1. A repentant lifestyle; make sure the Devil has nothing on you
2. Has a calling from the Lord in prayer and knows their assignment.
3. Knows how to get in their "place" or "location of prayer." free of distractions and the enemy interruptions.
4. Has a different kind of appetite for the meat of the Word.
5. Night warfare is for mature warriors, not for babes.
6. Has learned how to **stay wake/alert** in the night hours and use the tools of intercession: *discernment and discerning of spirits, listening, worship, communion (the Blood), prophetic declaration, teamwork, strategy sessions and united fellowship*
7. Delivered from the "spirit of convenience and comfort"
8. Developing their stamina and strength to pray longer and into the night
9. Not afraid of the dark or the night (stalkers, mental oppression etc.,)
10. Knows the Voice of God and the tactics of the enemy
11. Does not love sleep more than they love obedience to God
12. Quick to hear and obey the voice of God
13. Flexibility in their schedule and lifestyle to be used by God anytime
14. Delivered from the "clock"…
15. A keeper of secrets and revelation from the Lord
16. Open and teachable
17. Desires to know Jehovah Saboath (The God of War and the Head of Heavens armies)
18. Strong willed – does not give up or give in easily
19. Able to follow the "battle instructions" of the Lord without doubt/fear
20. Bold and courageous (not fearful of the enemy)
21. Not moved by "numbers" of warriors present
22. Realizes that the enemy does most of his damages at night
23. Knows the advantages of night warfare even if others don't
24. On Call 24-7 for the Lord and the Kingdom of God
25. Already is a "day warrior" and able to carry out a disciplined day plan
26. Must be delivered from the spirit of tradition and religion

The Advantages of Night Warfare and Night Warriors

(Read the Following Scriptures)

1. Divine Protection- Psalms 91:5
2. Ahead of Others- Proverbs 31:15
3. Special relationship with the Lord-Song of Solomon 3:1
4. God trusts you with a purpose and post – Isaiah 62:6
5. God reveals secrets to you – Daniel 2:19-23
6. We are prepared for the Accuser- Revelation 12:10
7. God speaks in the night. -Psalms 16:7

Remember:

Some battles take all night long and the victory comes just before dawn.

Weeping may endure for a night, but joy comes in the morning!

WEEK SEVEN- 5 Minute Review Quiz

Night Warfare-Night Warriors

1. List the seven things we learned from our Lord Jesus Christ as principles for dealing with night warfare. You may turn to Luke 22:39-46.

a. _____

b. _____

c. _____

d. _____

e. _____

f. _____

g. _____

2. List seven qualifications for being a Night Warrior

a. _____

b. _____

c. _____

d. _____

e. _____

f. _____

g. _____

WARRIOR LESSON 7

Nehemiah- A Night Warrior

Night Watchman- Night Warfare

Read and Discuss Nehemiah 2:11-18 and Nehemiah 4:15-23

Write down seven principles or key points we learn from Nehemiah about being a Night Warrior.

1.

2.

3.

4.

5.

6.

7.

Five Basic Principles from Night Warfare in US Military:

The United States military was defeated in many battles before they learned the value of night operations. They finally discovered that:

- 1. Soldiers must gird up their minds. It takes strong minds to do night operations, for the mind plays tricks on you in the dark.
- 2. Your vision or sight is not as clear at night, so you must have special devices to see at night. Do not fire on each other. Reorganize the darkness.
- 3. You become more fatigued at night because your body is used to sleeping and relaxing at night.
- 4. You must keep close contact at night. If not the other team members of the unit can get confused or tricked by the enemy and control is gone and the enemy can get the advantage.
- 5. For night operations to work, you must have strong leadership, training, planning and surprise tactics in your plans. Surprises make the enemy lose control and confuses the enemy.

What's holy and good about the Night?

- 1. God made the night and it is good
- 2. We are the light in the night
- 3. We don't have to fear the night
- 4. Night is time to sleep and rest also
- 5. God speaks in the night
- 6. Dreams and visions at night
- 7. Angles are on duty in the night
- 8. We've been given power to rule the night
- 9. Rescue missions occur at night
- 10. God executes judgment against evil
- 11. We can secretly survey the enemy's camp
- 12. God delivers His people in the night

13 Ways The Devil Affects the Night

1. The accuser is up day and night
2. The church is afraid at night- closed up and sleep
3. The law of God is not enforced 24-7
4. Magic and the occult is high
5. Thieves and robbers love the night and are at work
6. Sex, prostitution and crime flourish at night/in darkness
7. The church is deceived and untrained about night warfare
8. The underworld/gates of hell prevail at night
9. Terror is loosed at night and magnified at night
10. Unsaved men love the night/darkness
11. Rulers of darkness are ruling the night
12. Drunks are drunker in the night /Bacchus- god of intoxication is loosed full force at night
13. Satan has claimed "children of the night"

What other ways do you see that the Devil has affected your perception of the night even in your own life?

1. _____
2. _____
3. _____

What is meant by the terms below? Are the meanings positive?

Nightlife=_____

Night Club=_____

Night Riders=_____

Another Key Text: Lamentations 2:19

"Rise during the night and cry out. Pour out your hearts like water to the Lord. Lift up your hands to him in prayer, pleading for your children, for in every street they are faint and hungry." NTL

We must take the night back! How do we take the night back for the glory of God?

- **We must break off the fear of the night and darkness**
- **We must break off wrong teaching and wrong thinking about the night**
- **We must release a love for the night**
- **We must release a night watch anointing in the churches again**
- **Remember that night victories await us**
- **Remember that some victories have to take place in the night and just before dawn**
- **Declare the enemy will be defeated night and day**
- **Declare that Jesus Christ is Lord and Master over the night**
- **Declare we are called to night warfare and will win**

Our Lord Jesus had an active ministry in the night time.

- *Jesus walked on the water at night!*
- *Jesus sent angels to open the jails in the night!*
- *God gives dreams and visions in the night!*
- *Jesus was betrayed in the night!*
- *Jesus prayed in the Garden in the night!*
- *Jesus was arrested in the night!*
- *Jesus rose (before dawn) early Sunday morning, just before day with all power in His Hand!*

WEEK EIGHT- Five Minute Review Quiz
THINK TANK

Is God Trying to Make You A Night Warrior

1. What do you do at night when God wakes you up? Do you pray or do you eat and watch TV?

2. What fears do you need to be delivered from about the night?

3. Do you find it easy to stay up at night for everything else except prayer and Godly study? Explain.

4. What draws a person to be involved in a night club or have a night life? Maybe God anointed them as a night warrior but they may need to repent and give that "night gift" back to God.

WARRIOR LESSON 8

WOUNDED WARRIORS

When we are in the battle against spiritual darkness, trying to live right and obey and the Lord, it does not mean that we won't get wounded from time to time. There is no guarantee that warriors will never get shot at by the Devil or even wounded from their own soldiers which is called "friendly fire." **This first next section will be taught by Apostle Ivory Hopkins on <u>Wounded or Broken.</u>**

Wounded or Broken?

In the Bible we read about a "wounded spirit" and also about a "broken spirit." In some ways the meaning of these two terms is similar. Both terms indicate distress. It is possible even that one person may have a wounded spirit in response to the same situation that results in a broken spirit for another person.

But the two terms stand in contrast. First let's consider how they are used in Scripture.

"The spirit of a man will sustain his infirmity; but a wounded spirit who can bear?" **(Proverbs 18:14). The same Hebrew word is translated *broken* in**

Proverbs 17:22, where we read, "...a broken spirit drieth the bones." **The Hebrew word literally means "stricken." In both verses the NIV says "a crushed spirit."**

WHAT IS A WOUNDED SPIRIT?

A wounded spirit is one that is hurting, but one in which the hurt has festered into unbearable attitudes and responses. A person with a wounded spirit lives in inner misery that focuses regularly on his injuries.

Out of this focus come the following "unbearable" characteristics:

1. **A negative mind-set.** The person with a wounded spirit is preoccupied with past injuries. He views incidents in life in the worst light. He sees the bad and ignores the good. His mind is filled with woes, suspicion, and assumption of evil.

2. **Grievance mannerisms.** Out of a wounded spirit come sighs, groans, and exclamations that draw attention to the hurt. There is body language such as shaking the head, throwing dark looks, facial misery, and slumped shoulders.

3. **Blame tactics - Victim reasoning.** A person with a wounded spirit holds other people responsible for the misery in his life. In truth, others may have done him wrong, but those wrongs become the means of blaming others. The wounded spirit is able to cough up old injuries no matter what the present subject. The stories that are told put others in the worst light. In addition to direct blame, there are ways of insinuating--giving details in such a way that worse is implied.

Is it any wonder the proverb exclaims, "A wounded spirit, who can bear!" Out of the wound oozes the stench of self-pity, bitterness, and accusation.

In contrast to this is the broken spirit. "The sacrifices of God are a broken spirit: a broken and a contrite heart, O God, thou wilt not despise" (Psalm 51:17).

The Hebrew word translated *broken* is a strong word. It means "wrecked, shattered, even crippled or maimed." The Lord delights in the person with a broken spirit.

In Psalm 51, characteristics associated with such brokenness include:

1. *Acknowledgment of wrong.* A person with a broken spirit does not make excuses or blame others. He takes full responsibility for his wrongdoing.

2. *Contrition.* A broken spirit produces genuine sorrow.
3. *Humility.* Self-will has been shattered. There is no attempt to lift oneself up.
4. *Seeking after God.* The person with a broken spirit has faced his own poverty and sin. He has no righteousness of his own to promote, but rather, he seeks to know God.
5. *Teachability.* He is done with his own answers to life and is ready to turn to the Lord for help. He does not want his problem explained or justified; instead, he wants help to change.
6. *Unworthiness.* The person who is broken is spirit does not demand, he asks. His focus is not on getting all that he deserves because he knows he has been spared from what he really deserves. He is grateful instead of complaining. He has tasted mercy, and he is done with demanding rights.

Much as a wounded spirit makes a person difficult to live with, a broken spirit makes a person a joy to be around. He has a tenderness in manner, a gratitude for what others do, a humility about himself, and a gentleness in relating to others who have faults.

God heals the broken-hearted. He declares that He will dwell "with him also that is of a contrite and humble spirit" (Isaiah 57:15). When we experience brokenness and the blessings that follow, we wonder why we resisted such joy and freedom for so long. I am told that one village that received the Gospel for the first time and experienced genuine brokenness began the custom of greeting one another, "Do I meet you broken, brother?" Perhaps this would be a good practice to begin.

THE WOUNDED WARRIOR SURVEY

What are the ways we become wounded warriors?

Check off where you have become a wounded warrior or need help now with a wound.

1.___Critical and Unkind Words - Negativity and criticism can do more to wound and bruise the spirit than physical violence. Someone says something to you that "knocks you flat" and you can't get over it. Those words have penetrated deeply into your spirit in a hurtful, crushing kind of way.

> *"The words of a man's mouth are as deep waters"* (Proverbs 18:4).

> *"Death and life are in the power of the tongue . . ."* (Proverbs 18:21).

The old saying; "Sticks and stones may break my bones but words will never hurt me" is a dangerous lie. Words have spiritual values. They can create life in our spirit or they can produce death. "The tongue has the power of life and death" Proverbs 18:21.

2. ___Abuse- Abuse takes on three forms: verbal, physical and sexual.

Verbal abuse is a sad part of our culture. It is all too common to hear people making fun of and ridiculing children, spouses and one another. In spite of the intention, this still hurts. It is particularly harmful when it comes from those who are close, who instead should support and uphold.

"Scorn has broken my heart and has left me helpless. I looked for sympathy, but there was none, for comforters, but I found none" Psalm 69:20.

Physical violence is a major feature in entertainment; on television, videos and in the theatres. Media reports of real and wide spread physical abuses are forever before us. Young children are injured, wives are beaten and people are attacked on the streets.

"...the unfaithful have a craving for violence" Proverbs 13:2.

Sexual abuse, rape and incest are also major problems within our society. Because of the intimate nature of these forms of abuse, they are frequently concealed or denied. As a consequence the victims are denied justice and the guilty escape blame. To hide such abuses is debasing to the victims. In Samuel the story is told how Amnon, the son of David, became infatuated with his half-sister Tamar and raped her. In spite of her protestations, her brother, Absalom, convinced her to conceal the assault.

"And Tamar lived in her brother Absalom's house, a desolate woman" 2 Samuel 13:20.

In times of abuse there is a great need for support. If this is not forthcoming there is a strong sense of isolation. Without this support those, who are not at fault, frequently end up blaming themselves and languish in the guilt, which rightfully belongs to others.

3. ___ Sorrow or heartache is a damaging emotion.

"A happy heart makes the face cheerful, but heartache (sorrow KJV) crushes the spirit"
Proverbs 15:13.

Heartbreak is frequently the end product of an unfulfilled desire or craving, the outcome of unrealistic expectations, where another person or some material pursuit is worshipped or idolized. It can also be the result of an inability to forgive and let go of those who have sinned against us.

"The words of a gossip are like choice morsels; they go down to a man's inmost parts" (Proverbs 18:8, NIV). Those *"inmost parts"* are his spirit.

4. ___ SIN- Sin wounds us! When we put sin out of our life (through genuine repentance), we can be healed and restored body, soul and spirit is released to heal.

Sin is the curse of humanity! Sin is whatever comes between us and God! **It affects our spirit!** In Psalm 38 we read of David acknowledging a wounding in his life and spirit:

"Your arrows have pierced me, and Your hand has come down upon me ... there is no health in my body; my bones have no soundness because of my sin. My guilt has overwhelmed me like a burden too heavy to bear. My wounds fester and are loathsome because of my sinful folly ..." (Psalm 38:1-5, NIV).

"A wounded spirit who can bear?" David was hurting because of his guilt and consciousness of sin.

5.___Sexual immorality- Sexual immorality is a breeder of wounded spirits. Perhaps more people get wounded in this area of human relationships than anywhere else? Every wrong relationship can do damage to our spirit. The Bible separates sexual sins from all other sins (1 Corinthians 6:15-20). Christians are joined to the Lord as **"one spirit."** Sexual immorality joins us to the body of the other sexual partner. It is spiritual. **Sexual immorality affects every part of our being: spiritual, physical, emotional, our conscience and our mentality. It has the power to create another human being "in the image of God."**

"Flee from sexual immorality. All other sins a man commits are outside his body, but he who sins sexually sins against his own body" (1 Corinthians 6:18, NIV).

Regarding adultery, the Bible declares:

"But the man who commits adultery is an utter fool, for he destroys his own soul. Wounds and constant disgrace are his lot . . . " (Proverbs 6:32-35, TLB).

6.___Satanic Attacks- The thief comes to **"steal, kill and destroy"** (John 10:10). Satan loves to wound our spirit. He knows that when we carry a wounded spirit, we are no real threat to him. In Psalm 143:1-4 (KJV), David is crying to God because **"the enemy has persecuted my soul. He has smitten** ("bruised and wounded") **my life down to the ground . . . therefore my spirit is overwhelmed within me; my heart within me is desolate** ("laid waste" – Wilson's; "made numb, stunned, devastated" – Strong's)."

A wounded spirit brings down. It never lifts us up. Satan knows this. He wants us down! The Good Samaritan is a good example of knowing how to lift up the wounded. He knew what to do. He knew to pour in *"the oil and the wine."* Why? He identified with the wounded man's condition (Luke 10:25-37). Samaritans knew what rejection was, as *"the Jews had no dealings with the Samaritans"* (John 4:9). The man was restored.

7.___Rejection from Leaders- As this paper is written in the Christian context, we'll keep it to Church authorities - and other Christians. We have such high expectations of Leaders that when they fail us, or especially knock us back, or overlook us, it is easy for us to get discouraged and wounded. David experienced that rejection with King Saul (1 Samuel Chapters 18 to 31).

It also happens when Leaders promise certain positions to individuals – and then don't deliver, or they do not communicate the change of plan. Numbers get wounded when they are encouraged to go through training courses in order to be better prepared for church ministry, but at the end of the training it doesn't happen. Broken promises lead to broken hearts and wounded spirits. Some have been wounded trying to obey the Lord in the exercising of Spiritual Gifts and been "rebuked" or "cut down" publicly. Those "woundings" are hard to recover from, especially if one is sensitive and shy in the first place. Whatever the conflict or misunderstanding, don't hold a grudge against Leaders. Pray for them! Give them over to God. Give the hurtful "happening" over to God – release it from your spirit. Get healed of any wounding of spirit.

8.___Unforgiveness- With holding forgiveness from those who have disappointed and hurt us will "lock our spirit into" its wounding. We cannot heal if we do not release the hurt to God. 2 Corinthians 2:1-11 teaches us that if we don't forgive those who have caused us harm, Satan will take advantage of us. Let's not be ignorant of him wanting to get his "sticky paws" into wrecking our lives and future ministries that will impact the nations.

No matter how much someone has wounded us, we do have to come to a place of being able to release forgiveness to that person. If we don't, we will be the one who pays the highest price. We cannot afford to let anyone destroy us (because we can't or won't forgive) and therefore can't heal from the original damage caused.

"A crushed spirit who can bear?" (Proverbs 18:14, NIV).

In discussing this subject further (in a large group), we discovered some people have suffered a wounded spirit through the following:

9.___False Accusations- From time to time there are people who, for various reasons, have delight in making false accusations. Sometimes it is because of jealousy, sometimes it is just enjoying seeing one put down; other times ignorant gossip. Many false accusations have no affect upon us, but then there comes one that is "a bit close to the bone." It is directed at a loved one, or yourself, or your ministry. If we don't see those false accusations as being what they are – false! – we can take the accusation "on board" and it lodges in our spirit. We get wounded. This is where honesty is so important. We have to be honest with God, ourselves, and other people. If the accusation is false, keep it false. Don't give room for the enemy to "take us out" because we re-act wrongly. (If the accusation happens to be true, then we need to do something about it).

10.___Betrayal- This is indeed a very hurtful thing to work through, especially a betrayal of confidence. To be betrayed means "to disclose a secret or confidence treacherously; to break a promise, or be disloyal to a person's trust; to disappoint the expectations of" (Collins).

When the children of Benjamin and Judah sought out David in the wilderness, one of the leading questions he asked them was, ***"If you come to betray me to my enemies, seeing there is no wrong in my hands, the God of our fathers look thereon, and rebuke it"*** (1 Chronicles 12:16-17, KJV). David knew the power and hurt of betrayal, and he guarded against it as much as possible. Jesus warned there would be ***"many offended, and shall betray one*** *another"* (Matthew 24:10). The keeping of promises and confidences is very necessary if we do not want to be guilty of wounding our friends.

11.___Divorce- This is another "biggie," especially as it is so rampant in society today. To experience going from one extreme of being so in love with someone that you marry that person, and then to see it all change to the point where they can no longer love and live together, is a great tragedy. It affects the emotions, afflicts the mind, throws the children into turmoil, upsets the wider family and relatives, and changes the course of one's life. Rejection can become a huge issue. Many hurts are picked up. Attitudes are hardened. Later on, if those woundings are not dealt with and healed, the "baggage" from the broken marriage is carried over to a new relationship. Often the process repeats itself. More hurts and woundings eventuate.

12.___Relationships cut off through death of a loved one- The loss of a close loved one, relative or friend, can be a devastating blow. We all face the losing of someone to the death process. It is a sad fact that many people do not know how to relate to those who are suffering loss and grieving the death of a husband, wife, child, parent, close friend, etc. Our spirit, which is very vulnerable at that time, can be wounded by the words and actions of someone who doesn't understand what is going on inside the heart of those suffering loss. Sometimes the wounding happens because their close friends say and do nothing – just sitting in silence can sometimes be very hurtful. Other times people talk "rubbish" – or too much - and that can be equally hurtful. We need to be sensitive to the needs of those grieving the death of a loved one. If you're not sure, Ask! Don't let your friendship be cut off with those who grieve. Be mindful of the shock and "numbness" they're experiencing.

13.___Stolen Childhood- This was an interesting discussion. To listen to those who had experienced being the eldest child in a large family and being made to take major responsibility for all the younger brothers and sisters – while they themselves were still so young – brought about a wounded spirit. To expect a tender young life to do what it is not made to do at that stage of their development can only cause damage. That damage is carried through in attitudes that cause hurt in others. "Hurt people hurt people."

A wounded spirit comes into the lives of those children who are subjected to incest, prostitution, and other abuses (emotional, mental, physical, sexual, verbal, etc.). Many develop such a poor, low image of themselves that they feel the only way out is suicide. And it is no secret that the numbers of young people committing suicide today is very high!

13.___Unresolved grief (angry with God because you don't understand your situation)

There is a close association between unresolved guilt and physical & inner sickness.

"My guilt has overwhelmed me like a burden too heavy to bear. My wounds fester...I am bowed down and brought very low...there is no health in my body...even the light has gone from my eyes" Psalm 38:4-10.

I had occasion to counsel a 40 year old man who was confined to a wheelchair. He couldn't walk or feed himself. Prayer for healing brought no benefit. When asked what had happened 1-2 years before the deterioration in his body, his response was; "I slept with my best friend's wife." The guilt of that event had crippled him. Unresolved guilt makes our sins appear to be bigger than God's capacity to forgive.

Guilt is akin to the pain we feel when we put our hands into a flame. The pain warns us to take our hands out quickly before we are seriously burnt. Guilt is like this pain; it is a positive thing. Its role is to activate our consciences to our failures and to direct us to the Cross to receive forgiveness and cleansing. Guilt, that isn't resolved is this way, festers within our souls causing anguish and even physical suffering.

WOUNDED WARRIOR PREVENTION BY BISHOP DR. JACKIE L. GREEN

When you have a Wounded Spirit Don't....

- Repress it- You are the walking wounded. Do not pretend it didn't happen. Holding on to the wound is unhealthy and unwise. Don't hide it.
- Rehearse it- Do not go over and over it in your mind and torture yourself. Don't dwell on the You and again.
- Resent it (those that hurt you)- Resentment eats you up. It is called unforgiveness and bitter root. It is like cancer and sickness comes in with unforgiveness.
- Repeat it- Let there be wise gain from your pain. Don't fall into that trap again and again. Learn and also help others. Don't make the same mistake again.

Wounded Warrior SHOULD BE ...

- Repenting of it- Repent if you were deceived, ignorance, in sin or rebellion which caused you to be wounded. Repent of feelings of resentment toward those that wounded you.
- Renouncing it's power- Renounce Satan and let go of any anger, false pain killers, or anything that keeps giving the wound power over you. Renounce hidden things. Deal with the "power of pain" and take authority over it.
- Receive God's Peace- Let the Holy Spirit do his complete work and bring his healing and peace and love and wholeness into your life. Receive God's will and mind in your situation.
- Rely on God's Word to guide you and revive you. Spend more time with Him as He heals you.

Wounded Warriors Know they Are Healing When You Can:

- Pray for those that hurt you
- Love and respect your enemies
- Do good to those that wounded you
- Learn a life long lesson from that pain
- You are able to talk about it and testify and strengthen others
- The wound is a trophy, not a stumbling block. You have overcome it.
- Have power over it or them and you can be in the same room and not be affected by the past

ALL WARRIORS MUST GUARD THEIR HEART

"Keep and guard your heart with all vigilance and above all that you guard (your heart), for out of it flows the springs of life." (Proverbs 4:23)

*Close this class and PRAY for the wounded warriors.

WEEK NINE- Five Minute Review Quiz

1. **List seven things that cause a warrior to be wounded.**

   _____
   _____
   _____
   _____
   _____
   _____
   _____

2. **List five ways you know you are healing from your wounds.**

   _____
   _____
   _____
   _____
   _____

WARRIOR LESSON 9

Samson, the Weekend Warrior

Losing the Battle Behind Closed Doors

There are many of God's warriors who live a double life. They live one way in public and on the battlefield, but another way behind closed doors. Is that you?

If we are called to be God's mighty men and women warriors, we cannot be deceived into thinking we can be a "part time" warrior, partially holy and then lustful the rest of the time. Samson, chosen by God before his birth, a Nazarite, was to live a life as a warrior and judge for the people of Israel. There was no one like him, for God has endowed him with great physical strength. There were some serious problems that Samson was having behind closed doors. Today, we would call it a "hypocrite." *We are not called to be warriors just on Sunday, but the weekend belongs to God too.* Every day of the week belongs to God and we must be prepared and ready for battle. Let's read from Judges Chapter 16.

Judges 16:1-5

One day Samson went to the Philistine town of Gaza and spent the night with a prostitute. Word soon spread that Samson was there, so the men of Gaza gathered together and waited all ight at the town gates. They kept quiet during the nigh, saying to themselves, "when the light of morning comes, we will kill him." But Samson stayed in bed only until midnight. Then he got up, took hold of the doors of the town gate, including the two posts, and lifted them up, bar and all. He put them on his shoulders and carried them all the way to the top of the hill across from Hebron. Sometime later Samson fell in love with a woman named Delilah, who lived in valley of Sorek. The rulers of the Philistine went to her and said, "Entice Samson to tell you what makes him so strong and how the can be overpowered and tied up securely. Then each of us will give you 1,100 pieces of silver.

Judges l6: 17-18

Finally, Samson shared his secret with her. "My hair has never been cut, he confessed, for I was dedicated to God as a Nazirite from birth. If my head were shaved, my strength would leave me, and I would become was weak as anyone else."

Judges l6:21-22

So the Philistine captured him and gouged out his eyes. They took him to Gaza, when he was bound with bronze chains and forced to grind grain in the prison. But before long, his hair began to grow back.

PRINCIPLES OF THE WARRIOR SAMSON

As warriors for the Lord we must be aware of the enemy that wants to entrap us in our private lives. If we are not faithful in our private warfare and private lives unto the Lord, we will be exposed publically. Samson's private life behind closed doors was exposed. It cost Samson his eyes. What causes warriors to fall?

l. Every warrior has a "Delilah Spirit" assigned to their lives. *It is a spirit of seduction* (whether you are male or female you can be seduced) from your mission, and this spirit will not give up until the warrior is brought down, exposed and scandalized to mock the Name of the Lord.

2. Warriors must not desire the forbidden things. What forbidden things do you need to stay away from? Samson desired forbidden things and forbidden women.

3. Warriors must not take pleasure (especially behind closed doors) sin and those things that God has said is "of limits" to the warrior.

4. Warriors must not fall in love with those forbidden things/sins or anything that will weaken them as a warrior.

5. Warriors must not reveal their secret of their strength to the enemy. Don't let the enemy in and show the enemy your private places and places consecrated just for you and God.

6. Warriors must be alert and know when they are being set up by the enemy. Satan wants god's presence and power to left from our lives.

7. Warriors must guard their heart and their eyes. Samson lost his physical eyes because the Philistines gouged his eyes out. He had already lost his spiritual eyesight and Delilah took that.

8. Warriors have an enemy called "public scandal" that the enemy keeps in reserve for them. The enemy wants God's warriors to be disqualified and accused and exposed publically.

Discuss the Characteristics of the Weekend Warrior

- 1. The Weekend Warrior thinks they only need to show up on Sunday and the rest of the week they can live like they want to.

- 2. The Weekend Warrior lives an undisciplined life especially behind closed doors. They have not given up their secrets and confessed it to the Lord.

- 3. The Weekend Warrior is a "Sunday only" mentality and does not see the double lifestyle as a problem. They have lost the "fear of the Lord."

- 4. The Weekend Warrior is gifted but not wise. They have not learned how to walk in the fruit of the spirit. Fruit is more important than the giftings.

- 5. The Weekend Warrior does not like accountability and feels their private life is their own business.

- 6. The Weekend Warrior is deceived. They think because they are in the army, the other warriors don't discern they are half stepping.

- 7. The Weekend Warrior is a liability to the team and the whole operation. They are not sold out, but enjoying the grace and glory until it hits the fan.

- 8. The Weekend Warrior like Samson, is a target or weak link for the enemy. They are an open door to cause the team to lose the battle.

- 9. The Weekend Warrior thinks they know more than those in authority over them and even reject the instructions given to them by the Lord.

- 10. The Weekend Warrior would be better to "not be a warrior at all," until they are ready to commit fully to the Lord and to the war at hand. *We have enough weekend saints in the Church today.*

What are you doing behind closed doors that will cause you to lose the battles that are coming your way?

How does a Week End Warrior Get Renewed?--7 R's

- Repent- Is there unconfessed sins and do you need cleansing?

- Retreat- Get away with God…God wants quality time alone with us- Fall in love with Him Again…NO INTERRUPTIONS…When's the last time you got some time alone with God on a personal retreat?

- Refresh-Get strengthened by letting others pour into you; or take some time to feed yourself the Word of God.

- Recharge-Be filled with His Spirit/Holiness- Seek the Lord about being filled again with His Spirit and holiness. Fast and pray with passion like you used to.

- Refocus-Recommit fully: Get God's mind on every issue in your life and ministry. Are you so busy warring and doing things that you are out of touch with God? Are you hearing Him? Is your focus cluttered or off balance?

- Reposition-Fear the Lord: Make sure you are in the right place in this season and that you take very seriously God's commands.

- Reload-Get equipped and stock up on the spiritual resources you need in this next lap..Refill your tanks. What do you need to do to reload for the next battle that is coming? Has God been speaking to you about changes you need to make and what you need to reload?

Homework

Plan a 3- Day Spiritual Retreat for Spiritual Warriors

What would your retreat entail Friday Night at 7pm to Sunday Morning at 10 am. Use your imagination for the location and activities that will refresh the warriors. Use this one page below to list your schedule of activities.

Friday Night Retreat Begins

7:00 p.m.-

Saturday – All Day

Sunday- Concludes at 10a.m.

Closing Prayer

Prayer for the Weary Warrior
(Read each day this week)

Father, I thank you that I take regularly times to evaluate and ask God to search my heart to see if there be any contamination in me. I take an inventory of hidden sins and repent quickly of sins in my own life. I am quick to forgive others that have sinned against me. I make sure all my relationships in God are in order and all offenses are dealt with and dismantled. This includes my relationship with God first, then others. I remove myself from relationships if necessary or *guard my heart* with those that could contaminate my prayer life and I make sure all my relationships bring God glory. I am quick to obey the Voice of the Lord and repent when I have not been obedient. I check and make sure that my heart is soft and gentle and ready for God's use. I make sure no one has caused "hardening of the heart" to come upon me. I keep my regular quiet time and increase it as the Lord directs. I don't sacrifice my time with the Lord for other things. Because of the pressures of spiritual warfare, I have a regular "selah" or a *time(s) out* with God to get away from the routine and to get a fresh view of what God is doing and saying to me. I fast and pray regularly to keep my flesh under and to sharpen my spiritual discernment. I will make sure that I am scheduling ongoing deliverance to deal with demonic strongholds in my own life. I am submitted to a House of Prayer and have a church covering where God has sent and set me. I am open to correction and rebuke as well as compliments and encouragement from those that you have allowed to speak into my life. I find time to rest, sleep, laugh and play. I pray in tongues daily and increase it so that I will be built up in the most holy faith. I seek God for a fresh infilling of His Holy Spirit regularly and expect to be empowered to live a holy life for Him. I discern when I need to be anointed with fresh oil from the Holy Spirit. Forgive me for getting too busy to pray and not having balance in all things. I know I must guard myself against the spirit of prayerlessness and deception. I will stay in fellowship with believers of like precious faith and I attend corporate or group or church gatherings in prayer. I will stay focused on my prayer assignments from the Lord. I don't spread myself too thin. I will stay in my sphere of prayer and intercession and discern when a prayer assignment is finished and I am willing to move on to new assignments as the burden of the Lord is lifted. I keep journals on my dreams and visions, prophetic words, sermons, and any instructions from the Lord by keeping accurate records of what the Lord is saying to me from year to year. When I sense I am coming under attack, I spend additional time in praise and worship to saturate myself with His Presence. I thank you Father that I remember prayer and intercession is a privilege. It is a high and holy calling and it is the very ministry that our Lord Jesus Christ is performing right now at the right hand of the Father in Heaven. I recognize the oppression of the enemy coming against me now. I rebuke the powers of darkness over my mind and over my physical body. I take every demonic thought captive and cast down every lie, every spirit of unbelief and torment. I cover myself and especially my mind in the Blood of Jesus Christ. I rebuke and resist all heavy and unexplained oppression and depression, loss of concentration, feelings of spiritual deafness or comatose, withdrawal, sickness and backsliding spirits. I resist spirits of slumber, and break all curses being sent to me to hinder my prayer life and my effectiveness. Thank you Father that I overcome all attacks of the enemy by the Blood of the Lamb, the Word of my testimony and loved not my own life or self unto death. (Revelation 12:10) Holy Spirit I thank You for breaking the spirit of the weary warrior. Refresh me and restore the joy of my salvation. Create in me a clean heart and renew a right spirit within me. Shield me from the fiery darts of the evil one and hide me under the shadow of your wings. Renew my strength and fill me afresh with your precious Holy Spirit. For you are my Rock and my strength. You are my shield for me. You are the lifter of my head. In Jesus Name I pray, Amen.

(© 2010 by Bishop Jackie Green, JGM-Enternational PrayerLife Institute)

WEEK TEN-Five Minute Review Quiz

1. List three weaknesses that Samson had as a Warrior.
   _____
   _____
   _____

2. There are many "week end warriors" in the church today. List three ways you identify them.
   _____
   _____
   _____

3. List the seven ways for a warrior to get renewed.
   _____
   _____
   _____
   _____
   _____
   _____
   _____

4. What does it mean to not let the enemy take your eyes?
   _____
   _____

WARRIOR LESSON 10

How Warriors are Chosen

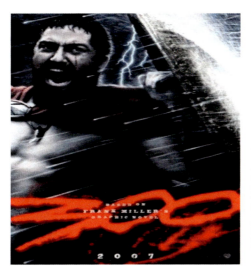

Gideon, A Warrior with a Reduced Army

(300 Spartans dvd)

(View and Excerpt from the Movie "Sparta 300" where King Leonardo meets the other warriors and they discuss what their profession are. The Spartans make it clear that a warrior is a full time position) What did you learn from this excerpt about warriors?

Three hundred is the spiritual number for "faithful remnant." Gideon had his 300 and the Spartans had their three too.

Read: Judges 7 (New International Version, ©2011

Gideon Defeats the Midianites

1 Early in the morning, Jerub-Baal (that is, Gideon) and all his men camped at the spring of Harod. The camp of Midian was north of them in the valley near the hill of Moreh. **2** The LORD said to Gideon, "You have too many men. I cannot deliver Midian into their hands, or Israel would boast against me, 'My own strength has saved me.' **3** Now announce to the army, 'Anyone who trembles with fear may turn back and leave Mount Gilead.'" So twenty-two thousand men left, while ten thousand remained.

4 But the LORD said to Gideon, "There are still too many men. Take them down to the water, and I will thin them out for you there. If I say, 'This one shall go with you,' he shall go; but if I say, 'This one shall not go with you,' he shall not go."

5 So Gideon took the men down to the water. There the LORD told him, "Separate those who lap the water with their tongues as a dog laps from those who kneel down to drink." **6** Three hundred of them drank from cupped hands, lapping like dogs. All the rest got down on their knees to drink.

7 The LORD said to Gideon, "With the three hundred men that lapped I will save you and give the Midianites into your hands. Let all the others go home." **8** So Gideon sent the rest of the Israelites home but kept the three hundred, who took over the provisions and trumpets of the others.

Gideon's Army of Warriors Had to Be Tested

Are you a Lapper or a Lagger?

<u>Lappers</u>

1. Consecrated
2. Concentration
3. Cooperation
4. Completion
5. Courageous/Fearless
6. Compassionate
7. Cheerful
8. Capable (well able)
9. Careful
10. Celerity
11. Champions
12. Charitable
13. Chief-front liners
14. Communicators
15. Commissioned
16. Committed
17. Confrontational
18. Confident
19. Consistent
20. Candid

<u>Laggers</u>

1. Contaminated
2. Comatose (sleepy/dull)
3. Conspiracy (betrayal)
4. Cantankerous
5. Cowardly (Send them home)
6. Callous (coldblooded)
7. Complainers
8. Counterfeit (when under pressure)
9. Careless
10. Celebrity spirit (self importance)
11. Competitors
12. Cheap (not a giver)
13. Childish (need to grow up)
14. Critical Spirit
15. Charmer (Flatteries)
16. Convenience
17. Complicated/complexities
18. Clickish
19. Corrupted
20. Cruel

Gideon was faced with the task of fighting the Midianites (Judges 7). They had large encampments, with women, children, cattle, camels and tents, which meant their greatest weakness was that they could easily be panicked by a surprise attack. This was exactly the strategy that Gideon chose to employ, which explains why he used such a small force of only 300 men. The smaller the force, the less chance there was of detection in a surprise attack. Gideon divided his troops into three companies and positioned one company on each of three.

Eight Principles for Every Warrior to Learn from Gideon

1. Every warrior must be tested for the battle. Each battle is different.

2. You can have "too many people" and that can cause you to lose the battle.

3. God is not concerned about numbers or quantity, but quality of the warrior.

4. Warriors can never be cowards. Send the fearful ones home.

5. Warriors must pass God's test. God sees further than man.

6. God will give you strategy for every battle

7. Warriors must give God the credit for every victory; we are just instruments.

8. The enemy will always test our faith and knowledge of the promises of God.

GROUP WORK

1. WHAT ARE SOME OF THE EXCUSES WARRIORS LIKE YOURSELF MAKE?

2. WHAT ARE SOME STRUGGLES YOU ARE HAVING BECOMING A SPIRITUL WARRIOR FOR GOD?

3. IF YOU DON'T GET IN THE FIGHT FOR RIGHTEOUNESS IN YOUR FAMILY, WHO WILL FIGHT?

WEEK Eleven-Five Minute Review Quiz

1. WARRIORS HAVE TO HATE THE ENEMY. DO YOU HATE THE DEVIL? List seven reasons that you hate the devil.

   _____
   _____
   _____
   _____
   _____
   _____
   _____

2. The spiritual number 300 means _____.

3. Gideon was a warrior who had his army reduced in force. Give three reasons Gideon's army was brought down to 300 by God.

   _____
   _____
   _____

4. Every warrior must be tested for battle. What three tests do you think warriors today need to pass before they can be considered "fit warriors for battle.?"

   _____
   _____
   _____

WARRIOR LESSON 11

Wise Warriors: Taking Territory Little by Little

Deut. 7:22—"And the Lord your God will drive those nations out ahead of you little by little."

Israel had enemies and they had to learn the principles of spiritual warfare.

God promised Abraham that he would be given the land of the Kenites, Kenizzites, Kadmonites, Hittites, Perizzites, Rephaim, Amorites, Canaanites, Girgashites, and the Jebusites (Gen 15:17-21). There are several lists of the peoples Israel will drive out of the land. There is a core of six peoples: Hittites, Perizzites, Ammonites, Hivites, Canaanites, and Jebusites. These six are listed in: Ex 3:8 & 17, 13:5 (omits Perizzites), 23:23, 33:2, 34:11, Deut 20:17, Josh 9:1, 12:8, and Judges 3:5. There is one shorter list of Hittites, Canaanites & Hivites only (Ex 23:28). Some lists add the Girgashites to the normal six: Deut 7:1, Josh 3:10, 24:11, Neh 9:8(omits Hivites)   (By Julian Spriggs, M.A.)

Israel knew their enemies and they had to pace themselves in order to overcome. They could not remove all the enemies at once. *Impatience is an enemy of the warrior.* These enemies are still with us today but in different forms. As I studied what these enemies presented, we can compare it today.

*Deuteronomy 7:1 When the LORD thy God shall bring thee into the land whither thou goest to possess it, and hath cast out many nations before thee, the Hittites, and the Girgashites, and the Amorites, and the Canaanites, and the Perizzites, and the Hivites, and the **Jebusites**, seven nations greater and mightier than thou;*

1. **Canaanites-***perversion/wickedness/occult/witchcraft*
2. **Amorites-***Idolatry, false worship/barbarians/like bees*
3. **Girgasites-***parasites/leeches on other nations*
4. **Hivites-***business/marketplace/mammon*
5. **Jebusites-** *Hard to conquer /Temple Mound today/Islam*
6. **Perizzites-** *mixture*
7. **Hittites-***paganism/new age/many gods/strong warriors*
8. **Philistines-** *A Thorn (Constant problem to keep Israel in check)*
9. **Moabites (Ammonites)-** *Blood Sacrifice/Abortion*
10. **Rephaim/Anakim-** *giants in the land/great/tall*
11. **Amalekites-** *revenge*
12. **Gaza-** *Bone of contention today/Gaza Strip & Israel*

What types of enemies (demonic spirits) are we warring against in America? List them here.

1. Idol of Mammon/Materialism/Money
2. Idol of Lust (for Power)
3. Idol of Self (lovers of self)
4. _____
5. _____
6. _____
7. _____
8. _____
9. _____
10. _____
11. _____
12. _____

Warriors do get weary. What promises did God give Israel back in the day... and also those same promises for His warriors today?

What is Spiritual Warfare?

Spiritual Warfare is = A _mature_ level of praying that confronts, overcomes and maintains righteous _authority_ over invisible demonic powers that hinder and blind people, regions and nations to the _Gospel_ of Jesus Christ.

Discuss why spiritual warriors must be in right relationships as prerequisite to Spiritual Warfare.

1. Right relationship with God
2. Right relationship with Self
3. Right relationship with spouse/family
4. Right relationship with pastoral and spiritual covering
5. Right relationship with church family/ relationships
6. Right relationship with community
7. Right relationship with governmental/marketplace

The Seven Levels of Spiritual Warfare

Discuss the types of spiritual warfare you are experiencing or will experience on each level.

1. Personal Level-_____

2. Family Level-_____

3. Church Level-_____

4. City Level-_____

5. State Level-_____

6. National Level-_____

7. World /Global Level-_____

For Homework Study the Warrior Scriptures in the Appendix.

WARRIOR 101
FINAL Take Home Exam

Directions: As a spiritual warrior, **choose one** of the areas of spiritual warfare you are dealing with. Write a four-six page paper, typed and doubled spaced, giving scripture basis and your own warfare strategies of how you are going to overcome the battle. Turn this in for the final class and be prepared to read and share it in class.

13 Dimensions of Spiritual Warfare

1. **Mental Warfare**– Warriors will experience a flood of vile thoughts, mental oppression, fear and doubt, forgetfulness, migraines, demonic suggestions and confusion. The voices of the enemy are strong and speaking continually to weaken the mind. *Is there an open door in your life? What's on your mind?*

2. **Physical Warfare**–Warriors will have unexpected attacks on the physical body, sickness, cancer, infirmities, fatigue, bruises, boils, and all kinds of strange physical attacks. The enemy doesn't want intercessors to learn how to rest, enjoy life, have fun and still be warriors. **The enemy seeks to keep intercessors —*overwhelmed, unbalanced and in a false transition.***

3. **Communication Warfare**- Demons attack the warriors in the area of communication lines so they won't be able to get instructions or talk to one another. Spirits of interference and blockage are sent to keep up confusion and break unity. The spirit of offence is sent to the intercessor so their actions or words are misunderstood toward one another. **The enemy wants the warrior displaced, disconnected and discouraged.**

4. **Relationship Warfare**– All relationships come under attack with warrior conflicts, betrayals, backbiting, turning on the ministry and one another, family problems and marital problems. Persecution and excommunication from other churches and friends is not unusual.

5. **Financial Warfare**– Warriors will be attacked in finances, job security, bank accounts, old bills arise from the past, garnishment of wages, stress on the church finances and unexpected expenses eat away at monies. Enemy will attack your faithful tithers and givers to cause them to leave the church or be attacked in their income. (Spirit of Python is sent to squeeze finances and resources to death)

6. **Emotional Warfare–** This warfare attacks the warrior's emotions and causes depression and oppression. The enemy brings up the past and strong condemnation. There are times of crying for no reason and even thoughts of suicide, death and failure thoughts. An emotional rollercoaster is released. Their dream realm and ability to concentrate is attacked.

7. **Temptation Warfare–** The Warrior is attacked in every "weak area" of their lives and tempted by the enemy to give up and go back to a lifestyle of sin and slavery. Pressure comes upon the intercessor and they feel unworthy beyond repair or that they cannot escape the enemy.

8. **Religious Warfare-**Religious spirits strongly attack WARRIORS/intercessors that have come out of tradition and religion. These spirits put pressure on the them to go back into the familiar traditions and try to convince them that they are in the minority. They are bombarded with "what people think" about their ministry and the accuser of the brethren spirits work together with religious spirits that are trying to regain control.

9. **Indirect Warfare-**Intercessors /WARRIORS MAY be not be attached directly all the time, but the attacks will come to their families near and far. These attacks are meant for the intercessor , but hits their spouses, children, co-workers or anyone connected to them that means a lot to them. This is called indirect assaults.

10. **Sexual Warfare–** Seduction (sex traps) and enticement is sent to seduce single or married intercessors. Perversion is sent to defile team members. Incubus and succubus spirits attack intercessors in their sleep with sexual assaults.

11. **Witchcraft Warfare–** Curses and attacks will be sent to those praying churches and spiritual warriors. The kingdom of darkness will attack anyone that is taking souls from Satan. Word curses, sorcery, divination and psychic prayers come against the ministry prayer ministry and the church. Intercessors are especially targeted.

12. **Territorial Warfare–** Intercessors/WARRIORS and the ministry/church will be attacked by the ruler spirits over the city and region. They will have to contend with hostile forces from the second heaven realm (Prince of the air), and they will experience extra warfare from the regional principalities and powers whom they are affecting and pulling down. Drastic changes in weather, environmental changes, natural disasters, accidents and such can be caused by these master spirits.

13. **Spiritual Development Warfare-**This warfare is released against the WARRIORS to keep them from studying the Word, worshipping, fasting and praying, carrying out their responsibilities and being on fire for the Lord! The enemy is throwing fiery darts constantly to keep the intercessor from being spiritually alert and spiritually powerful to carry out their God given commission from the Lord. They must not take shortcuts in their spiritual development or fall into excuses

WEEK TWELVE- Five Minute Review Quiz

1. **Define spiritual warfare**

   _____
   _____
   _____
   _____

2. **What are the seven levels of spiritual warfare**

   _____
   _____
   _____
   _____
   _____
   _____
   _____

3. **Name as many of the enemy nations of Israel as you can.**

4. **What does Deuteronomy 7:22 teach the spiritual warrior. (You can paraphrase)**

WARRIOR LESSON 12

/Becoming a Warrior Church

What is a Warrior Church?

A warrior church is a church or ministry that is called and commissioned by Jehovah Sabaoth (The Lord of Heaven's Armies) to a city, region or nation, to usher in the Kingdom of God by apostolically penetrating <u>demonic atmospheres, attitudes, alliances, associations, assignments, arsenals and abominations</u> of the kingdom of darkness with warfare worship, prayer, prophetic declaration, deliverance, preaching, wealth and revelation; until every knee bows and every tongue confesses Jesus Christ as *Lord and Savior; and the kingdoms of this world become the kingdoms of our Lord and Christ.*

Key text: Jeremiah 1:10 [10] **Today I appoint you to stand up against nations and kingdoms. Some you must uproot and tear down, destroy and overthrow. Others you must build up and plant.**

The six major operations of a Warrior Church is found in Jeremiah 1:10. A warrior church is first a praying and interceding church. Their intercession must be powerful to affect the region they have been called to. Share and give examples of:

1. Our prayers must root things out.

2. Our prayers must pull down strongholds.

3. Our prayer must destroy the works of darkness.

4. Our prayers will throw down.

5. Our prayer will build in the spirit realm.

6. Our prayers will plant.

15 Characteristics of the Warrior Church

(Pray that God will raise your church up to be a powerful warrior Church that strikes terror in the heart of the Devil and sets the captives free!)

1. *A warrior Church must be led by JEHOVAH SABAOTH --The Lord of Hosts. A warrior church is holy and sanctifies it's region, city or nation.*

<u>Is 6:3</u> ..."Holy, Holy, Holy, is the LORD (Jehovah) of hosts, the whole earth is full of His glory."

For thus says **Jehovah** *to me, "As the lion or the young lion growls over his prey, against which a band of shepherds is called out & he will not be terrified at their voice nor disturbed at their noise, so will the LORD of hosts come down to wage war on Mt Zion and on its hill. Like flying birds so the LORD of hosts will protect Jerusalem. He will protect & deliver it. He will pass over (pacach also describes the "Passover" cf uses in Exodus) & rescue it. (<u>Is 31:4, 5</u>)*

2. *A Warrior Church is visited and protected by angelic hosts and the fire of the Lord!*

3. *A Warrior Church is strong in apostolic and prophetic prayer and intercession/flowing in tongues and English.*

4. *A Warrior Church is strong in apostolic and prophetic worship, dance and prophetic acts, visions and dreams.*

5. *A Warrior Church is a strong "giving church" and has a mantle of wealth upon it.*

6. *A Warrior Church flows and releases God's revelation and knowledge of the Holy Spirit to affect lives, the region and nations.*

7. *A Warrior Church is a target for the fiery darts of the enemy through all forms of witchcraft and divination to stop the Kingdom work, therefore it is strong in casting out devils and healing ministry for those that are bound; as well as miracles, signs and wonders.*

8. *The Warrior Church sets a standard in the region they are called to and cause other churches in the region to be shaken and shifted back into God's biblical order.*

9. *The Warrior Church is passionate about children, youth, and the unborn generations being raised up to know their God and do Kingdom exploits.*

10. *The Warrior Church is a "gateway" to heaven from the earth realm to the throne of God, interceding for that which is on the heart of God and being an instrument of God's grace and mercy in the earth.*

11. *The Warrior Church is a day and night House of Prayer and a training center for multiple Kingdom venues and adventures to bring unity to the Body of Christ.*

12. *The Warrior Church is a Blood bought church, moving in God's power and authority of the Name of Jesus Christ, against the Gates of Hell, which will not prevail as long as there is a Warrior House that is Holy and obedient unto the Lord. There discernment and discerning of spirits is key in protecting the Church and the Body of Christ from deception and false teaching in every generation.*

13. *The Warrior Church is a birthing and travailing Church, that births in and mentors and brings forth leaders, ministries and those things that are in the heart of God.*

14. *The Warrior Church wars for the souls of men, women, boys and girls, as well as the soul of cities and nations.*

15. *Finally, the Warrior Church a priestly church, where the priest of the Lord gather to minister unto the Lord first. I Samuel 2:25 and II Peter 2:9*

Jehovah Sabaoth is the Strong Tower which God has made available for those times when we fail & are powerless, when our resources are inadequate, when there is no other help. And it is especially during those times that one comes to appreciate that God is truly the LORD of the armies & of all hosts. This comfort & confidence found in this Name.

Closing Article for Discussion by Rick Joyner (Morning Star Publications)

"There are many soldiers, but not many warriors," a Special Forces officer once told me. There are many professional soldiers who may take their jobs very seriously and be very good at what they do, but when you meet a warrior, you know the difference. Church leadership is about to be transferred from the hands of professionals, to the hands of true warriors, which the soldiers of the cross will all soon become. Warriors run to the sound of battle, not away from it. Warriors thrive in the intensity of conflict and danger. They are not discouraged by opposition or trouble, but rather come alive when faced with them. Such will be the constitution of the emerging generation of Christians. Those who think the emerging generation is soft will be shocked at the warrior nation that will soon be revealed.

God Is A Warrior

God is a Warrior. He uses the title "Lord of Hosts" or "Lord of Armies" ten times more than all of His other titles. He is a martial God. Those who are going to reveal Him in these times, are going to begin to take on the demeanor and discipline of a warrior, because the emerging generation is being prepared to serve in the greatest time of trouble the world has ever known. Even so, they will face those troubles with faith and confidence. They will earn the title "Overcomers" because they will never give way to opposition, troubles, or battles, but will fight to win like Joshua, who fought until the victory was total. These emerging warrior Christians will have this same resolve because they will know who they are, Who has sent them, and the power of the Kingdom that they represent. Like King David's mighty men, their exploits will be noised abroad and strike fear into the hearts of the enemies of the King. As this warrior generation emerges, it will impact and bring transformation to the body of Christ, which will be so profound, that churches will start being thought of more as military bases than congregations. Serious training and the sending out of spiritual forces for unprecedented strategic initiatives will become the order of the day.

Closing Reflection Questions

1. How will you respond to the attacks of the enemy as a warrior of the Lord?

2. What areas do you need to be more disciplined as a warrior?

3. Are you ready for more serious training so you can be sent out as a mighty warrior for the Lord?

4. How has this course helped shape you as a warrior for the Lord?

Prophetic Word for the Warrior Church

From Bishop Dr. Jackie L. Green

But beware as you pray and stand on your watch, for the Dragon shall come to eat the babies and those things that you have birthed and labored for. He shall even try and snatch those things out of your womb says God and abort the future. You must become fire fighters as you deal with the fire breathing dragon and flood specialist as the Dragon tries to drown thee. For you are my leather belts of truth that *will war with the dragon, the beast and the false prophets of your day.*

For in this next season it is not the hour of the mega church, but the mighty church!

Not the crowded church, but the "under the cloud church"

Not the arrogant church, but the apostolic church

Not the polite church, but the prophetic church

Not the popular church, but the persecuted church

Not the rich church, but the resurrection church

Not the traditional church, but the tested and tried church

Not the fearful church, but the faithful church

Not the worldly church, but the warrior church

Not the excuses church, but the eternal church

Not the prejudiced church, but the praying church

Not the frustrated church, but the fiery church

Not the greedy church, but the life giving church

Not the demonized church, but the deliverance church

Not the perverted church, but the proclaiming church

Not the poverty church, but the praising church

Not the bent over church, but the bold church!

APPENDIX

SCRIPTURES FOR WARRIORS OF CHRIST

Soldiers of Jesus Christ

2Ti 2:3 Therefore endure hardness, as a good soldier of Jesus Christ.

2Ti 2:4 No one who wars tangles with the affairs of this life, that he may please him who chose him to be a soldier.

The War Within

Rom 8:6 If our minds are ruled by our desires, we will die. But if our minds are ruled by the Spirit, we will have life and peace.
Rom 8:7 Our desires fight against God, because they do not and cannot obey God's laws.
Rom 8:8 If we follow our desires, we cannot please God.

Rom 8:13 For if you live according to the flesh, you shall die. But if you through the Spirit mortify the deeds of the body, you shall live.

Gal 5:16 If you are guided by the Spirit, you won't obey your selfish desires.
Gal 5:17 The Spirit and your desires are enemies of each other. They are always fighting each other

and keeping you from doing what you feel you should.

Gal 5:19 People's desires make them give in to immoral ways, filthy thoughts, and shameful deeds.

Jas 4:1 Why do you fight and argue with each other? Isn't it because you are full of selfish desires that fight to control your body?

1Pe 2:11 Dearly beloved, I exhort you as temporary residents and pilgrims to abstain from fleshly lusts which war against the soul,

Do not go forth quickly to fight

Pro 25:8 Do not go forth quickly to fight, lest you know not what to do in the end of it, when your neighbor has put you to shame.

First sit down and consult

Luk 14:31 Or what king, going to make war against another king, does not first sit down and consult whether he is able with ten thousand to meet him who comes against him with twenty thousand?

God will help you defeat your enemies

Deu 21:10 From time to time, you men will serve as soldiers and go off to war. The LORD your God will help you defeat your enemies, and you will take many prisoners.

Deu 20:1 If you have to go to war, you may find yourselves facing an enemy army that is bigger than yours and that has horses and chariots. But don't be afraid! The LORD your God rescued you from Egypt, and he will help you fight.

Jos 21:44 There still were enemies around Israel, but the LORD kept his promise to let his people live in peace. And whenever the Israelites did have to go to war, no enemy could defeat them. The LORD always helped Israel win.

Jer 1:19 And they shall fight against you; but they shall not overcome you. For I am with you, says the LORD, to deliver you.

God will fight alongside you and help you win the battle

Deu 20:4 The LORD your God will fight alongside you and help you win the battle."

Deu 7:21 So don't be frightened when you meet them in battle. The LORD your God is great and fearsome, and he will fight at your side.

Jos 11:6 The LORD told Joshua: Don't let them frighten you! I'll help you defeat them, and by this time tomorrow they will be dead. When you attack, the first thing you have to do is to cripple their horses. Then after the battle is over, burn their chariots.

Jdg 15:18 Samson was so thirsty that he prayed, "Our LORD, you helped me win a battle against a whole army. Please don't let me die of thirst now. Those heathen Philistines will carry off my dead body."

Pro 21:31 Even if your army has horses ready for battle, the LORD will always win.

Isa 63:1 Who is this coming from Bozrah in Edom with clothes stained red? Who is this hero marching in his glorious uniform? "It's me, the LORD! I have won the battle, and I can save you!"

The LORD goes out as a warrior

Isa 42:13 The LORD goes out as a warrior, He stirs up zeal like a man of wars; He shouts, yea, roars; He overcomes His enemies.

1Sa 17:47 Everybody here will see that the LORD doesn't need swords or spears to save his people. The LORD always wins his battles, and he will help us defeat you.

Rev 17:14 These will make war with the Lamb, and the Lamb will overcome them. For He is Lord of lords and King of kings. And those with Him are the called and elect and faithful ones.

The LORD gave him Victory in war

1Ch 18:13 Then he stationed troops in Edom, and the people there had to accept David as their ruler. Everywhere David went, the LORD gave him victory in war.

Jdg 3:10 The Spirit of the LORD took control of Othniel, and he led Israel in a war against Cushan Rishathaim. The LORD gave Othniel victory,

Don't Get Weary or Surrender to the Enemy

Isaiah 40:31— "But they that wait upon the LORD shall renew their strength; they shall mount up with wings as EAGLES they shall run, and not be weary; and they shall walk, and not faint"

Isaiah 54:17- No weapon that is formed against thee shall prosper; and every tongue [that] shall rise against thee in judgment thou shalt condemn. This [is] the heritage of the servants of the LORD, and their righteousness [is] of me, saith the LORD.

Put on the armor of light

Rom 13:12 The night is far spent, the day is at hand; therefore let us cast off the works of darkness, and let us put on the armor of light.

Put on the whole armor of God

Eph 6:11 Put on the whole armor of God so that you may be able to stand against the wiles of the devil.
Eph 6:12 For we do not wrestle against flesh and blood, but against principalities, against powers, against the world's rulers, of the darkness of this age, against spiritual wickedness in high places.
Eph 6:13 Therefore take to yourselves the whole armor of God, that you may be able to withstand in the evil day, and having done all, to stand.

Breastplate of righteousness

Eph 6:14 Therefore stand, having your loins girded about with truth, and having on the breastplate of righteousness
Eph 6:15 and your feet shod with the preparation of the gospel of peace.

Shield of faith

Eph 6:16 Above all, take the shield of faith, with which you shall be able to quench all the fiery darts of the wicked.

Helmet of salvation

Eph 6:17 And take the helmet of salvation, and the sword of the Spirit, which is the Word of God,

Weapons of warfare

2Co 10:3 For though walking about in flesh, we do not war according to flesh.
2Co 10:4 For the weapons of our warfare are not fleshly, but mighty through God to the pulling down of strongholds,
2Co 10:5 pulling down imaginations and every high thing that exalts itself against the knowledge of God, and bringing into captivity every thought into the obedience of Christ;

Fight the good fight of faith

1Ti 6:12 Fight the good fight of faith. Lay hold on eternal life, to which you are also called and have professed a good profession before many witnesses.

1Co 9:24 You know that many runners enter a race, and only one of them wins the prize. So run to win!
1Co 9:25 Athletes work hard to win a crown that cannot last, but we do it for a crown that will last forever.
1Co 9:26 So then I run, not as if I were uncertain. And so I fight, not as one who beats the air.

2Ti 4:7 I have fought the good fight, I have finished the course, I have kept the faith.

Be strong in the Lord

Eph 6:10 Finally, my brothers, be strong in the Lord and in the power of His might

Suggested Reading List for Warriors

Anderson, Neil, *The Way of Escape, Freedom from Sexual Strongholds*.

Annacondia, Carlos, *Listen to Me Satan!, Exercising Authority Over the Devil in Jesus' Name*, Creation House.

Archibald, Dr. Pam Crowder, *The National Diabolical Construction of Slavery, Racism, and Church Division*, Copyright by Dr. Pam Archibald, Phoenix, AZ, 2004.

Baer, Randall, *Inside the New Age Nightmare*, Huntington House, Inc., Lafayette, LA, 1989.

Barclay, Mark, *Sheep, Goats and Wolves*, Mark Barclay Ministries, 1985.

Barna, George, *What You Need to Know About Today's Youth*, Regal Books, Ventura, California, 1995.

Bernal, Dick, *America Spiritually Mapped*, Jubilee Christian Center, San Jose, CA, 1994.

Brown, Michael, *Revolution, The Call to Holy War*, Renew Books, Ventura, CA 2000.

Chavda, Mahesh & Bonnie, *Watch of the Lord*, Creation House, Lake Mary, Florida, 1946.

Clark, Jonas, *Seducing Goddess of War*, Spirit of Life Ministries, Ft. Lauderdale, FL.

Damazio, Frank, *The Gate Church*, City Bible Publishing, Portland, Oregon, 2000.

Damazio, Frank, *The Making of a Leader*, B.T. Publishing, Portland, Oregon, 1988.

Daniels, Kimberly, *Clean House, Strong House*, A Practical Guide to Understanding Spiritual Warfare, Charisma House, Lake Mary, Florida, 2003.

Dawson, John, *Healing America's Wounds*, Regal Books, Ventura, California, 1994.

Dawson, John, *Taking Our Cities for God*, Creation House, Lake Mary, Florida, 1989.

David, Jonathan, *Apostolic Strategies Affecting Nations*, Johor, Malaysia, 1999.

Dyrness, William A., *How Does America Hear the Gospel?* William B. Eerdmans Publishing Company, Grand Rapids, Michigan, 1989.

Eastman, Dick and Hayford, Jack, *Living and Praying In Jesus' Name*, Tyndale House, Wheaton, IL, 1988.

Eckhardt, John, *Demon Hit List*, Whitaker House, New Kensington, PA, 1995.

Eckhardt, John, *Moving in the Apostolic*, Renew Publishing, Ventura, CA, 1999.

Eckhardt, John, *Leadershift, Transitioning from the Pastoral to the Apostolic*, Crusaders, Publications, Chicago, IL.

Eckhardt, John, *Identifying and Breaking Curses*, Crusaders Publications, Chicago, IL.

Eckhardt, John, *Prebyteries and Apostolic Teams, Crusaders* Ministries, 2000.

Fletcher, Kingsley, *I Have Seen the Kingdom*, A Revelation of God's Final Glory, Creation House, Orlando, Florida, 1998.

Gibson, Noel and Phyl, *Evicting Demonic Intruders*, New Wine Press, West Sussex, England, 1993.

Gibson, Noel and Phyl, *Excuse Me Your Rejection is Showing*, Sovereign World, Kent, England, 1992.

Gilbert, Martin, *Winston Church Hill's War Leadership*, Vintage Books, NY, 2003.

Goll, James W., *Praying for Israel's Destiny,* Chosen Books, Grand Rapids, MI, 2005.

Goll, James, *The Seer*, Destiny Image Publishers, Shippensburg, PA, 2004.

Grant, Bernard, *First Class Leaders*, *Fifty Principles for Becoming a Strong Leader,* Milestones International Publishers, 2004..

Hammond, Frank and Ida Mae, *Pigs in the Parlor*, A Practical Guide to Deliverance, Impact Books, Kirkwood, MD 1973.

Hammond, Frank and Ida Mae, *Our Warfare Against Demons and Territorial Spirits,* The Children's Bread Ministry, Plainview, TX, 1991.

Hammond, Frank and Ida Mae, *Children's Deliverance*, Impact Christian Books, Kirkwood, MD, 1996

Hambrick, Stowe, *Charles E., Charles G. Finney, and the Spirit of America Evangelicalism*, William B. Eerdmans Publishing Co., 1996.

Harris, Jack, *Freemasonry*, Whitaker House, New Kensington, PA, 1936.

Harari, Oren, *The Leadership Secrets of Colin Powell*, McGraw Hill Publishers, NY,NY, 2002.

Hendricks, William & Howard, *Building Character in a Mentoring Relationship As Iron Sharpens Iron*, Moody Press, Chicago, IL, 1995.

Haugk, Kenneth C. *Antagonists in the Church, How to Identify and Deal with Destructive Conflict*, Augsburg Publishing House, 1988.

Hopkins, Apostle Ivory, *Deliverance from Evil Soul Ties*, A Handbook for Breaking Difficult Bondages Related to Soul Ties, Royal Creations, Harbeson, DE.

Hopkins, Apostle Ivory, *Deliverance from Marriage Breaking Spirits*, Pilgrims Ministry of Deliverance, Harbeson, DE.

Hopkins, Apostle Ivory, *Deliverance from Damaged Emotions*, Royal Creation, Harbeson, DE, 2000.

Hopkins, Apostle Ivory, *Deliverance from The Draining Spirit*, Royal Creation, 1998.

Horrobin, Peter, *Healing Through Deliverance*, Book I, Sovereign World Press.

Horrobin, Peter, *Healing Through Deliverance*, Book II, Sovereign World Press.

Illnisky, Esther, *Let the Children Pray, How God's Young Intercessors are Changing the World*, Regal Books, Ventura, CA 2000.

Jacobs, Cindy, *Women of Destiny*, Regal Books, 1998.

Jacobs, Cindy, *Deliver Us From Evil,* Putting A Stop to the Occult Influences Invading Your Home and Community Regal Books, Ventura, CA, 2001.

James, Kay Coles, *Transforming America from the Inside Out,* Zondervan Publishing, Grand Rapids, MI, 1995.

Joyner, Rick, *Overcoming Racism,* Morning Star Publications, Charlotte, NC, 1996.

Joyner, Rick, *Overcoming the Religious Spirit, Combating Spiritual Strongholds Series*, Morning Star Publications, Charlotte, NC , 1996.

Joyner, Rick, *Overcoming Witchcraft*, Morning Star Publications, NC, 1996.

Kelly, John with Costa, Paul, *End Time Warriors*, Renew Books, Ventura, CA, 1999.

King, D.E., *Preaching to Preachers*, Neibauer Press, Warminster, PA, 1984.

Koch, Kurt, *Occult Bondage and Deliverance*, Kregel Publishers, Grand Rapids, MI, 1970.

Lardie, Debra, *Concise Dictionary of the Occult and New Age*, Kregel, Pub, Grand Rapid, MI, 2000.

Layton, Dian, *Soldiers with Little Feet*, Destiny Image Pub., Shippenberg, PA 1989.

Liardon, Roberts, *God's Generals* I, Albury Publishing, Tulsa, OK, 1996.

Liardon, Roberts, *God's Generals II,* Whitaker House, New Kensington, PA, 2003.

Liardon, Roberts, *Breaking Controlling Powers* , Albury Publishing, Tulsa, OK, 1991.

Liardon, Roberts, *Sharpen Your Discernment*, Albury Publishing, Tulsa, OK, 1997.

Liardon, Roberts, *Smith Wigglesworth: The Complete Collection of His Life*, Albury Publishing, Tulsa, OK, 1996.

Liardon, Roberts, *Apostles, Prophets and Territorial Churches* (Six Tape Set), Roberts Liardon Ministries, Laguna Hills, CA.

Lockyer, Herbert, *All the Men of the Bible,* Zondervan, Grand Rapids, MI, 1958.

Lockyer, Herbert, *All the Women of the Bible*, Zondervan, Grand Rapids, MI, 1958.

Morgan, Dr. Patricia, *How to Raise Children of Destiny*, Destiny Image, Shippensburg, Publishers, 1994.

Scott, Brenda and Smith, Samantha, *Trojan Horse, How the New Age Movement Infiltrates the Church*, Huntington House Publishers, Lafayette, LA, 1993.

Servello, Pastor Mike, *God's Shield of Protection*, Mt. Zion Ministries, 2003.

Silvoso, Ed, *Prayer Evangelism, How to Change the Spiritual Climate*, Regal BOosk, Ventura, CA, 2000.

Silvoso, Ed, *That None Should Perish, How to Reach Entire Cities for Christ Through Prayer Evangelism*, Regal Boosk, 1994.

Smith, Alice, *Beyond the Veil, God's Call to Intimate Intercession*, SpiriTruth Publishing, Houston, Texas, 1996.

Stevens, Selwyn, *Signs and Symbols, Cult, New Age, Occult Insignias and What they Mean,* Jubilee Resources, New Zealand, 1999.

Towns, Elmer and Porter, Douglas, *The Ten Greatest Revivals Ever from Pentecost to the Present,* Servant Publications, Ann Arbor, MI, 2000.

Pierce, Chuck D. and Sytsema, Rebecca, *The Best is Yet Ahead*, Wagner Publication, Colorado Springs, CO, 2001.

Pierce, Chuck D. and Sheets, Dutch, Releasing the Prophetic Destiny of A Nation, Destiny Image Publishers, Inc., Shippensburg, PA, 2005.

Pierce, Chuck D. and Sytsema, Rebecca, *The Future War of the Church*, Regal Books, Ventura, CA 2001.

Price, Kenneth, *The Eagle Christian,* Old Faithful Publishing Co., Wetumpka, AL, 1984.

Powell, Colin, *Leadership Secrets of Colin Powell*, McGraw Publishers, 2003.

Rainer, Thomas S. *The Bridger Generation*, Broadman-Holman Publishers, Nashville, TN, 1997.

Trimm, Dr. Cindy, *The Rules of Engagement, Book I and II,* Cindy Trimm, Corporation Ft. Lauderdale, Florida, Strang Communications, 2005.

Vallowe, Ed. F. *Biblical Mathematics, Keys to Scripture Numerics*, Vallowe Evang. Association, Forest Park, GA< 1991.

Wagner, Doris, M. *How to Cast Out Demons, A Guide to Basics*, Renew Books, Ventura, CA, 2000.

Wagner, C. Peter, Editor, *Territorial Spirits*, Sovereign World Limited, England, 1991.

Wagner, C. Peter, *The New Apostolic Churches*, Regal Books, Ventura, CA 1998.

Wagner, C. Peter, *Confronting Powers, How the New Testament Church Experienced the Power of Strategic Level Spiritual Warfare,* Regal Books, Ventura, CA 1996.

Wagner, C. Peter, *Apostles of the City, How to Mobilize Territorial Apostles for City Transformation,* Wagner Publications, Colorado Springs, CO, 2000.

Wagner, C. Peter, *Prayer Shield, How to Intercede for Pastors, Christian Leaders and others on the Frontlines* (The Prayer Warrior Series), Regal Books, Ventura, CA 1992.

Wagner, C. Peter, Church Quake, *How the New Apostolic Reformation is Shaking Up* the Church as We Know It, Regal Books, Ventura, CA, 1999.

Wentroble, Apostle Barbara, *Prophetic Intercession*, Renew Books, Ventura, CA, 1999.

Wentroble, Apostle Barbara, *A People of Destiny, Finding Your Place in God's Apostolic Order*, Wagner Publication, Colorado Springs, CO, 2000.

White, Randy, *Church Without Walls, God's Blueprint For the 21st Century Church*, Creation House, Orlando, Florida, 1998.

Wilkinson, Bruce, The Dream Giver, Multnomah Publishers, Sisters, Oregon, 2003.

Worley, Win, *Witchcraft Workings in the Church*, Win Worley Publications, Mesquite, TX, 1990.

Worley, Win, *Rooting Out Rejection and Hidden Bitterness*, Win Worley Publications, 1992.

Worley, Win, *Conquering the Host of Hell*, Win Worley Publications, 1981l.

Worley, Win, *Annihilating the Host of Hell*, Book I, Win Worley Publications, 1981.

Calling God's spiritual warriors! The battle is raging!

If God has made a promise to you, you will have to learn to war for it. Your promised land is a target for the enemy.

You've got to identify what you have that the enemy will fight you for. This is why the *warrior spirit* is crucial this hour in order to fulfill the promises and purposes of God for your life and future generations.

Strap Up Your Boots!

This course will stir you, strengthen you, settle you and send you forth to battle!

About the Author

Bishop Dr. Jackie L. Green *is an apostle and a warrior set in the Body of Christ to bring raise up armies for in the Body of Christ. She is the wife and life partner to Pastor Anthony Green for 45 years and she is committed to equipping the saints for the work of the ministry. She is the founder overseer of JGM-Enternational PrayerLife Institute and Rapha Deliverance University. Her numerous prayer education tools can be ordered through JGM-National PrayerLife Institute.*
VISIT; www.jgmenernational.org. or authorhouse.com or amazon.com.

Made in the USA
Las Vegas, NV
09 January 2025

16145819R00071